# ANGELS
## AMONGST US

*Our Journey*

*Angela*

**BALBOA**
PRESS

A DIVISION OF HAY HOUSE

Balboa Press books may be ordered through booksellers or by contacting:

Balboa Press
A Division of Hay House
1663 Liberty Drive
Bloomington, IN 47403
www.balboapress.com.au
1 (877) 407-4847

Because of the dynamic nature of the Internet, any web addresses or links contained in this book may have changed since publication and may no longer be valid. The views expressed in this work are solely those of the author and do not necessarily reflect the views of the publisher, and the publisher hereby disclaims any responsibility for them.

The author of this book does not dispense medical advice or prescribe the use of any technique as a form of treatment for physical, emotional, or medical problems without the advice of a physician, either directly or indirectly. The intent of the author is only to offer information of a general nature to help you in your quest for emotional and spiritual well-being. In the event you use any of the information in this book for yourself, which is your constitutional right, the author and the publisher assume no responsibility for your actions.

Any people depicted in stock imagery provided by Thinkstock are models, and such images are being used for illustrative purposes only.
Certain stock imagery © Thinkstock.

Print information available on the last page.

ISBN: 978-1-5043-0355-2 (sc)
ISBN: 978-1-5043-0356-9 (e)

Balboa Press rev. date: 08/02/2016

# *Acknowledgements*

*I* give my sincerest thanks to all my family and friends who have given me the inspiration to write this book.

To my Reiki Master/Teacher who taught me so well with her sincerity and love.

My beloved husband who has always allowed me to spread my wings, and supported me in all that I do.

# Introduction

This book started out as my own personal journal through life, yet as time went on I realised that by others reading these experiences it would help them to recognise the similarities and strengths you each have as individuals within yourselves and the trials and tribulations you will, or have experienced, do end in time.

It is my belief that each of us have Archetypes or themes to work through in this life and the four main ones are CHILD (wounded) SABOTEUR (when you want to achieve and you keep telling yourself that you can't) PROSTITUTE (selling yourself short not acknowledging your own values and VICTIM (why me). Once we learn the lesson, we then put them in a place of love and move on.

This book has been ongoing for over eighteen years, however over the past two years have had the re-occurring thought to get it finished. It was while we were away staying with relatives in Europe that I had a dangerous fall down some stairs and broke my wrist, although looking back now I realise that it could have been a lot worse. This subsequent quiet time allowed me the inspiration to finish the book albeit with my left hand at first, then using my fingers of my right hand once it had strengthened.

So enjoy and feel inspired about our journey through this life and know that whatever happens to us it is not by coincidence, chance or luck. Any accidents that happen to us our Angels are there to soften the blow. Know that we are been watched over and looked after at all times.

I would like to add that all the names are fictional, to protect the people that help make this book possible.

# Childhood

$\mathcal{A}$ s I sit here at the computer, glancing out over the ocean I realise how far I have come. At 69 years of age I can look back on my life and understand my journey. I am content and at a place of peace. I am grateful for what I have learnt through my experiences, gaining self-acceptance, wisdom and the deep desire to share and hopefully inspire others. This is my journey...

In my early childhood, we lived at my paternal grandmother and grandfather's terrace house north of London, England.

# Nanna

$\mathcal{N}$anna, as we called her was a very gentle lady who was kind and a loving. When she was young she was slim and very beautiful, but what I remember about Nan was that she was plump and in her sixties. Each morning I would get up and go downstairs where she would usually be standing in the kitchen with a small mirror on the wall, tending to her hair. Her hair was long and white and she would pain-stakingly roller a piece at a time with a metal wand, that she would then place a hairgrip through one end and then a piece of hair about an inch in the metal grip and begin to roller it up to the top of her head, once this was complete it would be released to unveil the perfect curl. Her legs would swell as I remember her shoes were laced in the front and her feet would swell over them, as you can tell I loved her to pieces and still do.

One particular time that comes to mind is when I was around 3yrs old and being intentionally naughty and said the word "bugger". I succinctly remember the more I was told to stop, the more I said it. Nan threatened to put soap in my mouth to stop me swearing, she gave me plenty of warning but as children do, I pushed her to her limits. Until eventually she chased me with a bar of soap, (*it was called Fairy and anyone with an age similar to mine will remember it was a large dark green bar of soap*) I ran away laughing until Nan cornered me behind a chair and proceeded to put this bar of soap in my mouth. With my teeth clenched so tight, Nan rubbed against my teeth, boy did that leave a taste in my mouth and I can assure you I never swore again. It was around this time, my mother and grandmother became concerned by the way I walked. To them it looked like I had one leg shorter than the other, they called in the doctor who laid me on the table and measured my legs, then said I was fine. Although some years later when my bones had stopped growing, is what eventually led to a hip replacement. My memories of living with Nan were very special as we had lots of fun together, we would tease one another in a playful way and those were happy times that will be forever held in my heart.

Something very fitting for the era and another fond memory of mine was of my Nan knitting. She would always make sure that we had plenty of warm jumpers and cardigans to wear, with the aid of our outstretched hands holding the yarns of wool which would then be wound into balls ready for knitting. As my dad and granddad were fishermen, mending hob socks (as they were called) was a regular occurrence, as there were plenty of socks to mend! Washing used to take a full two days on both a Monday and Tuesday. The washing would be hung around the black lead fireplace with a brass fender. I can still see my mother and Nan cleaning it and the radio playing 'The little red train came over the hill and she blew'.

In front of the fireplace was a homemade rug, which would be made up of old coats and any heavy materials that were cut into strips and weaved together with a special hook. I used to love to smooth my hands over the rug, it was really quiet beautiful in my eyes

At this time I had only one older brother, whose name was Mark. Mark was four years older than myself and about seven years of age, he had dark hair and blue eyes and was quite tall in my eyes. As a younger sibling I looked up to him, although unfortunately we didn't play together very often, looking back I guess I was somebody who was a bit of a nuisance to him. One particular time we were playing in the back garden, which was narrow with a brick wall about three and a half feet high all the way round and a gate that opened into a passage way, as all back to back terraces homes did in those days. Mark was spinning a stool with metal legs around and around and I happened to accidentally get in the way, unsurprisingly the stool then collided with the right on the side of my face, with my ear taking the worst of it. It was many months after the accident that my ear would cause me pain, until eventually I became ill and had to spend some time in bed it was after the doctors visit that I was diagnosed with having a Mastoid in my ear and was told that eventually later in life it would cause deafness. The doctor made arrangements for me to go into hospital, however the day before I was due to be admitted it miraculously burst. This was to be my first encounter of the power of healing energy, however at this early age I wasn't to know that. While spirituality is now embraced and consciousness is growing, back in the 1950's it was largely misunderstood, almost feared by some. It wasn't until later in my life that I was made aware of an Aunty who, living in Australia, was a spiritual healer. Her path wasn't directly discussed in my family for the above reasons, however I am now aware she was the one sending me distant healing.

At the age of about two/three my dad bought me a dolls pram, a miniature Silver Cross model and it was beautiful. Shiny black in colour with giant silver wheels and etched motifs on either side. I knew my mother wasn't happy about this at the time after overhearing her complaining it was too big for me. While she may have been right, it was truly beautiful and eventually I grew into it and loved pushing it around with my doll inside.

I am about four years old now, they say you don't remember things but I distinctly remember having to go to Sunday school wearing a bright red bowler hat made of felt. I never liked wearing hats, and to this day still don't. I tried to protest. But nobody listened, I am only a child what do I know what I want? I thought to myself that if I hide the hat hopefully they won't find it! Opening a side cupboard I pushed and squeezed the hat right to the very back, it was so small that I made sure it wouldn't be seen. Sunday came around and as expected my mother and Nan were looking frantically for my treasured hat, *(because of course you can't go to Sunday school without one!)* Then, much to my dismay, they found it! It was pushed into shape, straightened and pressed firmly on my head and away we went.

My older brother Mark had a two wheeler bike and when he wasn't using it, he would lean it against the wall, temptation was great as I didn't have bike. One time when he was out (*and any given chance*) I would climb on the bike and have a little ride round in the garden. This became a regular habit of mine, I couldn't reach the seat, so standing on the pedals was my only way of riding it. Unfortunately my foot would slip sometimes and would bang my bottom so to speak on the cross bar. One day when my granddad was in from sea, mum, nan and granddad were all dozing in chairs. I was sitting on my mother's knee feeling a bit sleepy, when mum said to me "Go and sit on your granddads knee". Climbing down off mum and nestling on my granddad's lap he said, "You shall have your bike my dear" in his dozing state. This was a complete surprise for me, as I really wasn't expecting to hear those words. It was not long after that he took me to the bike shop. We chose a bike together, it was red, and I loved it. Granddad paid for the bike with three big five pound notes, I remember they were white with black writing on and the shop smelled of fresh rubber.

Before I reached the age of five, my mother wanted me to go to school, I overheard the discussion between my mother and Nan. I heard my Nan say "Don't you think she's a bit young you May?" in her gentle north English accent. This in turn, planted a seed in the back of my mind. When the day came for me to go to school the first thing I saw were big heavy iron gates, I was taken in and left. As I walked along the corridor, I felt so small and everyone looked bigger than me. Playtime came and all I could think was that I am too young. Using both hands and all my strength to open the big iron gate, I ran across the road, through the passage and home to Nan's house. Walking in the back door, and the notable surprise on their faces said, "What are you doing home?" My answer to this was of course, "I am too young".

# *Grandad*

*My* granddad was a wise, quiet and gentle man who was very easy going. On reflection, I suppose he had to be with all the comings and goings that went on in his home, they never had any time to themselves.

My mother and grandmother would hope that the men would not be in from the sea at the same time, as there was so many of us. My Nan, granddad, dad, my mother, elder brother, myself and our uncle. I would sleep with my mother if dad was away and with my Nan if granddad was away.

I remember once sleeping in nan's bed and the next morning, whilst I was still asleep she came upstairs with a cup of tea and some bread and butter on a plate, I felt so special that day and it's still a heartfelt memory even now. A favorite time was when dad or granddad would come in from sea with their neckerchief (usually worn around their necks) full of shell fish, tied at the top and bursting from the sides. Everyone would gather in front of the fire and using any hard handled tools that could be found, crack the shells open to expose fresh, white flesh full of flavor.

Granddad who was my dad's father fought in both World War One, which they say was one of the worst wars, sleeping in ditches filled with water, and World War Two.

During World War Two my grandfather was a skipper fishing off the north sea when he encountered a Nazi Heinkel directly attacking the trawler he was captaining, on not one but three separate occasions. It was this direct action against the enemy plane that resulted in a life changing decision for him as at this time the only defense he had available to him, was a rusty rifle. The first time was for twenty five minutes, the second time six weeks later for seventy minutes and the third time a few weeks later for thirty six minutes. What led to this action was that at first they were all below deck as they watched this Heinkel firing bullets which ripped into the deck of the trawler puncturing the hull. Terrified screams rang out in the silence as the Heinkel overhead turned and roared past again, as the pilots machine gun belched out hundreds of bullets and smashed into the bow of the stricken trawler.

Suddenly my granddad who was quite small in stature appeared on the deck, a middle aged man in waders ran to take hold of the only defense they had, a rusty old rifle. As the crew were frantically urging him to get below for his own safety. At that moment he looked up and unleashed six shots in quick succession, as he bore down cracking open the barrel to reload. This startled the pilot of the Heinkel as the bullets stung his cockpit which made the Heinkel turn and flee. Later on that day as things started to settle down, he notice his lapel in his jacket had a hole in it, when he opened the jacket there was an indenture from a bullet in a metal tobacco case that he carried. It was this experience that then led my grandfather to join the Royal Navy as part of the war, which my father also served.

He was later awarded an M.B.E (Member of the British Empire) for his bravery whilst on the fishing trawler, receiving a written acknowledgement from Winston Churchill.

Both my father and my grandfather fished for all their lives. As granddad got older he ended his days as cook on board the trawler unable to bear the cold outside because of his rheumatics, a remnant of his service of fighting in world war one.

Unfortunately for dad he finished his fishing days at the age of fifty eight. This being forced upon him, as the fishing industry declined due to the fact that Iceland extended their fishing limits and our fishermen were no longer allowed to fish in their area. This combined with the decline of fish available for trade meant all the fleets weren't making enough money to keep it all up and running and eventually were all sold off to different parts of the world. Mostly to Spain and Australia.

Last year I saw my father's old ship the Saxon Onward as my husband and I were out walking along the local wharf. My father had spent eleven years on the one ship and although it was brand new at the time, the memories came flooding back. I remember it so well, and it was a really good looking trawler. Sometimes, if the tide times were in our favour we would go down to the lock gates and wave to dad as he was stood on the bridge, returning from his time at sea. Once he had passed us, we'd watch the trawler head for the pontoon where they would be docking, then off we went rushing of to see my Dad on the ship. On special occasions, and once the crew had disembarked were allowed on. One time I was about six months pregnant and climbing aboard dad held my hand very carefully to make sure I didn't slip. It was looking at that same trawler now that I felt overwhelmed by emotion of all those memories of my father. Mike and I decided to take a closer look and we spoke to the man who was preparing the boat ready for the next trip. He offered us the opportunity to come aboard and have a look around, but sadly I declined as I just wasn't ready at that time. The next day, Mike and I returned once I was feeling more able to cope with the emotion and climbed aboard, seeing how much it had changed. In its glory of the mid 1960's with its freshly polished wooden deck, she was a brand new trawler, polished black on the outside with white rim on her stern and bow, it was a far cry from the rusty blue coloured vessel before me. It was all iron and steel, the inside was nothing like I remembered, it was quite sad to see it in its old age. The cabins were run down, the galley no longer recognisable and wheelhouse that was had been replaced by modern technology. It now fishes mainly between Tasmania and Australia and I've seen it a few of times since.

# Leaving My Grandparents Home

$B$ack to my childhood and living at my grandparents' home.

We lived there until I was five years old and as mentioned I had grown very close with my Nan. It could be at this point that you question the lack of information relating to my mother. To fill in some of those gaps, she was small in stature and well-rounded and had a strong personality. Many mothers of her age were very similar, and I wondered if the war had something to do with it. My mother was raised by her grandparents as her mother died after giving birth to her, some say she lost the will to live as her husband never treated her well. Shortly after, my mother's older brother (who would have been three at the time) is said to have died pining after his mother.

My younger brother Pete was born when I was four years old. I remember my Nan making a bed out of the large bottom dressing table draw. It wasn't long after Pete was born that we moved to a new council house. Unfortunately, I never really settled there and missed my Nan so much and would visit at any given opportunity that I could.

In all I had three brothers an elder brother Mark, myself together with two younger brothers one four years younger, named Pete and my youngest brother Graham. Graham was born when I was eleven years of age. When Graham was born my father delivered him at home one morning. There was myself and my younger brother Pete busy getting ready for school and our eldest brother Mark had already left. I noticed that mother was just moving about restless and sitting on different chairs and dad was waiting for her to decide whether to go in the maternity home. But unfortunately my mother left it too late. The next thing I knew was that my father went upstairs and dragged my single mattress down and threw it on the floor, then telling me to go next door with my younger brother. It wasn't long after that, that the ambulance arrived and carried my mother and the new baby Graham on a stretcher. Dad had safely delivered his new son into the world and made sure my mother was safe too.

As Graham grew I became more confident with him so would help my mother, occasionally feeding him, changing the odd nappy as I remember trying to be careful not to stick the safety pin in his manly regions, even bathing him in the kitchen sink. I grew to feel like a little mother towards him. It was also hard for my mother especially when one of us would become sick. One time when my youngest brother Graham had Scarlatina my mother came to my bedroom woke me up and asked if I would look after him whilst she had one decent night's sleep, (dad was away at sea at the time) so I climbed in the cot with him. I do however, remember mother saying that Graham wouldn't be seeing our Nan as much as the three of us did, we just loved our Nanna to bits, a gentle lady who would never intentionally hurt anyone as she saw good in everyone. I didn't realise it then but my mother, bless her, was a very jealous person. During this time my father was away at sea ten days out of fourteen and on stormy nights I have known my mother to pace the floor worrying about him.

It wasn't easy for my mother I know, but my feelings for her became very uncertain shortly after moving into our new home, I was five years old at the time. A little girl had just moved in next door and was also five years old, although I was older by one month. As during that time we weren't privileged with lots of new age gadgets as they have now, and rarely spent time indoors we were playing outside, making our own fun in the garden. She was in hers and I was in mine, with just a chicken wire fence dividing the houses and the grass was quite high. As we sat on the grass we began to innocently throw stones over the fence, not knowing where they would land as neither of us could see the other properly. The next thing I knew was hearing her run screaming into her mother, leaving me to assume one of my stones may have hit her. Within what felt like seconds, my mother came running out, grabbed hold of me by my arm and dragged me all the way upstairs she would not let me explain, she just was not listening. There was a large high cupboard in the small spare bedroom room and she lifted me up and locked me in it. This would be an extremely frightening experience for anyone, but for a five year old especially so. It was pitch black and I was so afraid I screamed and sobbed for what seemed like an eternity. When she did eventually lift me out of the cupboard, my feelings for her were different, unfortunately from that day on I was very unsure of how I felt towards my mother or indeed how my mother felt about me.

As time went by and whenever people came to visit she would make me out to be an awful child. Whenever her friends would arrive and talk to me out of politeness, I would respond to them in the same respectful way. However, my mother would repeatedly time and time again say 'you don't know her' indicating that I wasn't who I appeared to be, which was not the case and as an innocent child it was these remarks that hurt me so much. The only way to describe how this felt to me was a deep dread in the pit of my stomach, internalised.

The same question I would always ask myself over again was "Why is my mother like this towards me, and what have I done so wrong that she hates me the way she does?" It seemed as though the boys could do no wrong and even if the eldest lied, she would believe him. To me it was though if I tried to tell her the truth there was no way she would believe me, I would raise my voice in tears and she would threaten that behaving in that way would see me end up in a mental institution, as my Aunty had. It was my hopelessness and despair at being misunderstood and that truth never seemed to matter to her. Mark, my eldest brother would play on this and would stand behind mum with a grin on his face. Whenever I tried to speak my truth I always had to raise my voice to try and get her to listen to me. By the time I reached the age of twelve and started to feel more grown up (yet still being threatened to be put in a mental institution), it was becoming too much to bear and I started to question how much more I could take. My father was the one I could always talk to and it was one day when he returned from sea that I decided to tell him about what was happening, as up to this point he had no idea. It was as I started telling him and releasing all of my hidden emotion that I broke down and sobbed. Dad was so hurt by all this that he told my mother that he didn't ever want to hear that sort of talk in this house and for that time, she stopped.

What I have come to learn and understand is that all emotion can be felt internally and held within each chakra, the stomach being all that relates to your individual one to one relationships. At the time for me, this needed healing. Clearing the blockages created by my relationship with my mother and it's this hindsight now that helps me to better understand her as woman, on her own personal journey. One of my mothers' friends would visit and she started to say how nice it was of me to trim the Christmas tree. That's when mother would say negative things about me I was becoming more and more hurt, until I slowly rose to my feet and left the room and went quietly upstairs feeling sick to my stomache and crying. Our cat would be in my bedroom who became my confidante and councellor dad rescued him off the ship he sailed his mother had rejected him similarities to mine as there is no such thing as coincidence,

I look back now and realise it was all a part of my journey. And that journey is what has made me who I am today. It was the start of my soul's growth.

I was painfully shy when it came to mixing with others and really had to make a conscious effort to step out of my comfort zone. I never really settled when we moved from my grandparents' house at the age of five. Therefore I would visit my nans house at every given opportunity, I loved just being there, and I felt safe.

As I was growing up, I had one or two close friends at school, Liz being my best friend and still is to this day, even though we now live twelve thousand miles apart some things never change.

*Age 12*

$\mathcal{I}$t was when I was twelve years old that granddad was admitted to hospital and diagnosed with cancer and was told he had six months to live. I remember thinking that he had not long retired from the sea, this was their time for one another.

Grandad came out of hospital, and life was as normal as it could be. My grandparents would come on the bus to our house for visits. It was on one of these visits that they were returning home on the bus, that Nan collapsed whilst on the bus suffering a severe stroke. It was to be some time before she returned home, but granddad prepared everything for her return even moving the bed downstairs, as they lived in a terraced house with steep steps, it made it easier for both of them.

Nan had been home about a week and with granddad looking after her, I was concerned so offered my help. One day at the age of twelve I ventured to their house with the aim of cooking them dinner, it was to be steak in the oven even though I had not attempted this before. To my surprise it turned pretty well for a first attempt, in all I don't think it mattered, I just wanted to help. I was greatly disappointed with my mother at this time, as I've noted we lived with my grandparents for many years, yet in their time of need my mother claimed to be too busy when previously she had made time to take us there twice a week for a meal before Nan had the stroke.

I always felt that she could have done more for my grandparents and although my mother had granddad stay with us when my Nan passed over, ten years later it didn't feel enough.

Seeing me get married and my baby daughter who was about six months old at the time. I remember her looking at me with her beautiful sad eyes and saying "I never thought I would live to see this moment" Unfortunately it was to be only nine months after moving in with my mother that granddad joined my Nan. He died of a heart attack, not the cancer. Looking after Nan until she passed away and then he was ready to go himself. My parents and grandparents have all passed over now, and I am not so young myself anymore.

## *Leaving School*

*L*eaving school at fifteen, my best friend Liz and I decided we both wanted to be hairdressers, as at that time everyone wanted to be a hairdresser. We got on our bikes and rode around town to as many different hairdressing salons as we could, putting down our names at each one should a vacancy arise. Ultimately, none ever did. In the end I got a job in a department store and Liz in a confectioners. It wasn't long before Liz met her future husband and it was then we lost contact. Liz married at nineteen, myself at twenty, only bumping into one another on rare occasions. Firstly when we had both had our first baby's and then again outside my mother's house in the area where we both grew up.

Work was a means to an end and shoes were certainly not my passion, however I did have a creative side and was given the chance to become a window dresser and train in London. My lack of confidence wouldn't allow me to make such a move and with a potential engagement on the horizon, I used that as my excuse. It was around this time that for no apparent reason my wrist began to ache and lose strength, the emotional meaning is not knowing which way to turn, but I didn't know that then. I tried to understand why this was happening, but there was no known cause.

My excuse for not leaving for London was a man by the name of Bryan, whom I later married. He would drive past our house in his green Morris Minor which had a white painted top. I was once standing at the front gate talking with a friend, and he drove past in his car with a friend named Keith, Keith knew me from school and lived just around the corner. After about five minutes Keith walked up the street and asked me if I would go out with his friend, Bryan. I wasn't sure what to do, but eventually, as I knew Keith and he assured me it would be alright I said yes. I was sixteen, a bit nervous especially as he had a car, but it turned out alright. We would go out perhaps two or three times a week. Then one day we broke up, the reason being he was worried about what his friends thought, claiming we were getting too serious.

I would go and visit Nan on Sunday's and remember asking if I could live there, because to me it was the only place I felt happy and could be myself.

My Nan declined although she would have loved to have me there, she was afraid of any tension or rift it might cause with my mother. I was so disappointed and never forgave Nan and as time went on I said some hurtful things to her, which upset her, and to which I regret to this very day.

Self-forgiveness is one of the hardest emotions to overcome, most people will forgive you, but forgiving yourself is very difficult and needs to be worked with, this was my first experience of this.

Time went on and I would go dancing with my friends, we loved to dance and sing and I met someone else, Kevin was his name, he was skinny and had a motor bike. We went all over on that bike and would talk for hours, becoming good friends and it was nice. It was at this time that Beth (the girl next door) was a bit lost for things to do and we introduce her to Kevin's friend Barry. Beth and Barry eventually married some five years later.

In life we will each encounter many 'sliding doors' moments. One such moment of mine was one night being out dancing with friends and as we were leaving, Kevin came over and offered me a ride home on his motor bike. I declined as I was with friends and Kevin left. Shortly after, Bryan who had broken up with me a month earlier, approached in his car and offered us all a lift and being as we could all fit in his car I said yes.

After taking everyone else home Bryan and I ended up chatting and eventually again becoming an item. Those days were quite different, marriage was something people expected in early years and with Bryan being nineteen, he explained he didn't want to get married until he was twenty five. That didn't bother me as I wasn't ready anyway, but discussed getting engaged on my eighteenth birthday. Which we did.

# *Engaged*

*A*t eighteen I became engaged, I wasn't happy at home and thought that I would be able to make my own happiness. Life was black and white back then, or so I thought as most people do at that age. Plus, I also thought that I had plenty of time to change my mind before the day arrived so wasn't overly concerned. My approach to the whole thing wasn't what you would expect of a young person in love. I was reluctant to set the date as I hadn't even thought about it, even though others continued to ask.

Two weeks into the engagement the man with whom I was engaged to marry knocked on our front door and as I opened it, he calmly told me that he had booked the church. The decision had been taken from me and I knew I should have felt excitement, but instead had a sinking feeling and resigned myself to fate, 'what will be, will be. On our first Christmas together after the engagement Bryan came to my home to give me a present, it was very heavy and needed to be held with both hands. Excited I rushed to open it with Bryan wishing me a Happy Christmas as I did. Much to my dismay, inside was a huge frying pan. Shock and disappointment doesn't begin to explain my feelings, in hindsight I should have hit him on the head with it!

The wedding was booked for two years in the March just after my twentieth birthday. I changed jobs although continued to sell shoes in a smaller store. What followed for me was an emotional fight with my heart and my head questioning whether getting married was really something I wanted to do, a mental tug of war fighting against my intuition. Eventually I collapsed in the shop where I worked unable to move my eyes I could hear what was happening around me, but couldn't speak and not able to move a muscle. I was carried around the back of the shop and laid on some chairs with my manager trying to give me some water. I was very aware of what was going on, but unable to do anything about it. Eventually after what seemed to be an eternity I came round.

A couple of days later I was crossing the road and glanced down and saw some sort of small brass figure, I picked it up and took it home with me. I am not sure what made me carry it home, however later found out that it was Joan the Wad, a figure of luck. This was symbolic in itself as at this point in my life, felt I needed all I could get.

As well as Sunday's, I used to visit nan and granddad's most Friday lunchtimes in my break from work. I was eighteen by this time and would often take with me butter, eggs and some other essentials. On one occasion even taking over some lace curtains as with my nan now living downstairs felt she needed more privacy. Still at eighteen I was aware of how my mother perceived me and would be sure to ask nan not to let her know the things I did for them. I had accepted how she felt about me and didn't feel the need to have her change her mind. Grandad would often sit at the kitchen table during my visits and I would go and sit with him for ten minutes, before I went back to work. He would be sat at the kitchen table reading the newspaper and I would just listen to him read the articles out loud. It was on one of these occasions that he said something to me so profound, that it had an effect on me for many years to come.

These were his words:

He said "I'll tell you something my dear because you listen to me"

"You know, I knew I had only six months to live all those years ago, (six years ago) but the mind is a very powerful thing. I would imagine that some very tiny people would be working and chipping away all the disease that was in my body". Keeping this up as long as he felt it necessary.

This was a beautiful, intelligent man who I will forever admire.

# Twenty Years Old

$\mathcal{E}$ngaged now and about to be married my future in-laws seemed to take over life and I let them. They found us a house and came to help me decorate, while their son 'my future husband' kept working to save. He rarely visited to see how things were coming along and never had any real involvement or input with getting it ready, and his parents took care of everything. He was the only child and his mother always made a fuss of him, as his father once pointed out whilst I was waiting for him to come home from work at their house.

He hadn't arrived home until 8.30pm, however his mother at this time was prepared to make him whatever he wanted. Reeling off a menu for him to choose from. All the signs were there yet I still did not listen.

The wedding date soon arrived, and I was due to be married at 1pm. As the taxi arrived, I stood with my father by our fireplace, a glass of sherry in hand when my father turned to me and said "It's not too late to change your mind", my immediate response was, "It is you know!".

The wedding went ahead and in my heart of hearts, I thought love would come. But sadly it never did.

I later found out that on the day of the wedding, whilst the photos were being taken and unbeknown to me, my mother turned around to my mother-in-law and said "I hope she has three like herself!" It was at this point my mother's best friend turned to my mother-in-law and said "Let me tell you that Angie is a very nice girl!" Unfortunately as my nan was too unwell she couldn't make it to my wedding, after the reception I went to visit her at home. We were taken by car and showed her what I looked like in the wedding dress and her eyes lit up and it was a beautiful moment for me.

I fell pregnant almost straight away and my daughter Amanda was born 10 months later and my world felt complete, I adored her I would sit by the fireside on a pouf and sing to her for what seemed like hours and she would just gaze up at me always smiling.

My twenty first birthday came around and I was sat in a chair giving Amanda her bottle, when I noticed a taxi pull up outside the house. To my surprise it was my mother who had dropped in as she didn't want me to spend my birthday alone. This meant a lot to me, especially considering our past relationship.

Amanda grew into a very kind and considerate person who will gladly give her last to help anyone, she has a wisdom beyond her years. Her passion is working with children and helping people, always a ready smile for all and children take to her very easily, as do adults. One of life's eternal givers, giving of herself without expectations of others.

A few years later my second daughter was born and during the pregnancy I decided she would be named Diane. I went into labour in the early morning and upon my husband arriving home at lunchtime, needed to decide whether it was time yet to leave or not. He was going back to work and no labor, nor new child was going to stop that. He dropped me off at the maternity home and there I had a second beautiful daughter. As I gazed at my second daughter, I decided that the name I had picked didn't suit her and instead settled on Jane. Different to my first born, Jane gave me a look that said she wasn't happy to be here, yet to this day I feel that Jane is much misunderstood. When my mother came to visit she was over the moon. I was to find out there and then that it was the name of her grandmother who brought my mother up from birth who was also named Jane.

As Jane grew older she had the most beautiful golden blonde hair and brown eyes which was unusual for a fair skinned person. The girls were as the expression goes, chalk and cheese. Jane has a strong personality and would often win if her and her sister were arguing. For example being the youngest she would go to bed first and the eldest followed later. Half an hour later after the eldest went to bed, she would come down upset saying Jane won't let her sleep, this was a regular occurance no matter how firmly you talked to her and tried to cojole her nothing worked. I used to worry about her constantly, because even as a small child she was closed. When she was about six years old, I remember sitting on her bed with her talking to her all afternoon, trying to get her to open up, but to no avail. It really saddened me because my children are important to me and you just want them to be happy.

While I previously mentioned what happened to my mothers mother and older brother, I missed the part about her father. Unfortunately he was also absent from my mothers life. He too was a fisherman and was often away, yet made little/no effort to see her when he returned. When my mother was 12 she was introduced to him on street while shopping with her grandmother, no introduction and little warning other than "This is your father". As he aged I do remember him coming to our home when we were in our teens and in my eyes he seemed a very old man. He would often bring her a bar of chocolate on arrival which was generally thrown on the windowsill. I don't know whether my mother resolved her feelings towards her father, but she never refused him a meal.

# Early Twenties

$\mathcal{D}$uring my early twenties, I noticed that my leg would give way, but never enough to cause any great concern. It was not long after giving birth to my second daughter, that I experienced severe back pain and was unable to put my left foot on the floor without experiencing terrible pain in the bottom of my hip and back. As mothers do however, I soldiered on and tried do the best for my children while putting any initial thoughts of myself on the backburner. I was twenty four before I saw a specialist for the pain. On examination I was told I had a collapsed disc, put in a corset and told not to do any bending however with two small children this is not an easy task. Not long into wearing the corset I was busy tidying up and momentarily forgetting the advice I had been given, bent down to pick something up and felt an immense pain in the bottom of my back and in turn had collapsed another disc.

Help from a higher source

Pain was a part of my life now going about doing my usual shopping at my regular market stall, I was chatting away to a man who regularly served me, when he noticed something wasn't right with me and brought a lady friend along to see. They were a part of a healing group and while not together romantically, they did work together. On looking at me she said she believed I needed help and asked if it would be possible to come round to my house to perform a healing. While apprehensive at first I was willing to give anything a try that could potentially help me to feel better. The next week they performed the healing at my home which provided me with a boost. I saw them once more but this was the beginning of something which left an imprint on my subconscious and would prove invaluable as time went on. Looking back now, I realise I had consistent nudges towards spiritually, the power of the mind and energies after the initial conversation with my granddad back when I was 18.

When my youngest daughter started school at 5 years old, I decided to think about doing some type of work that I knew I would enjoy. Plus considered the money would come in useful to buy some much wanted new furniture. After giving it some thought, and putting aside any previous disc problems I decided to take an entrance exam to become a nurse. At the back of my mind though, were my young children who were only five and eight years old and even after passing the exam I had my doubts as to whether it would offer the needed balance in raising them. When questioned by the head nurse if I believed this was the right time to enter a career, I honestly answered no. This lead to my working part-time auxiliary rather than full time nursing.

Working as a part time Auxiliary Nurse gave me great satisfaction, as I was able to balance work and children. Unfortunately over time my neck was damaged through the heavy lifting and affected my shoulders and arms so I had to give up the nursing as I knew I couldn't lift anymore.

What followed next was visit to an orthopedic surgeon and eventually a visit to hospital for manipulation to put the discs back in place, but unfortunately it was just a quick fix and the problem with the discs reoccurred again within the week.

Diagnosed with Cervical Spondylosis at the age of thirty, I was filled with fear of what my life may look like at 40. As it was I was barely able to make it out of bed, crawling around on all fours and using heat lamps on myself to loosen my limbs and get moving for the day. The pain was unbearable. I would go to bed in the afternoon to be pain free as it was relieved when I was laying down, although it's hard to admit I reached a point where dying felt like a better option than having to live in constant pain. It was during one of these afternoons I had a very vivid dream. Struggling on my hands and knees, trying to climb this lush green hill that I just couldn't reach the top, no matter how hard I tried. There were men dressed in white robes with their backs to me and as much as I kept reaching out they just wouldn't turn around. A psychic later informed me this was communication from the other side that it wasn't my time, and while I didn't know what at that point – I still had work to do.

On my visit with this same psychic she gave me the name of a healer in London whose name was Mr. Edward Fricker. She knew little else, other than that he worked in London so the rest was up to me. After finding his address at the local library I wrote him a letter introducing myself, explaining my situation and my history over the last 10 years with a request to see him. He replied to my letter and put me on a healing list for three months, asking me to pray to be healed each night at 10pm. I did as I was directed and each night at the same time prayed to be healed. As I did I would experience a warm sensation down my spine. When the time arrived for me to go and see him in person the following March, I booked the train and with a map took myself off to London not knowing where I was going. Once I arrived in London I took out my map and caught the underground from Kings Cross to Oxford Circus where I found his office, full of hope and anticipation of what might lay ahead I made my way inside. With his wife working on reception, I confirmed my arrival and took my place in the waiting room. Looking around it was really very interesting to see all types of people from all walks of life, walk in and out the small office with only one treatment room. Two men whom I can only describe as looking like they worked for the government entered the waiting room and being double parked expected to be seen straight away. As they didn't have an appointment they were turned away as not one person was more important than another.

When it was my turn to see Mr Fricker, I was greeted by a lovely gentleman who spoke the whole time asking me questions whilst smoothing his hands from my head to my feet whilst I stood in the center of the room. I remember it being comfortably warm in the room with a green leafy plant standing over a meter tall in the right hand corner. It was as though he could read my mind and I succinctly remember his reassurance that if my own faith was waning to not be concerned as he had enough for the both of us. He then explained that to think of him as a battery that was golden and asked me to touch my toes. This to me was an impossible task as I hadn't been able to in nine years. On the third time he asked me I bent down and touched my toes and could not believe how I felt, tears of joy filling my eyes and my whole being.

On my second visit and looking into Edward Frickers eyes, it seemed that for one nanosecond those eyes changed, and at that moment those eyes gave me a feeling of such I can only describe the word humbleness. I was so small in the scheme of things yet uniquely as important. On the same day he gave me two A3 sketches of Jesus and was told this is the nearest to His likeness. I have never experienced before and haven't since that split second I was in the presence of someone very special indeed, the feeling was that of Jesus and I will be eternally grateful for what I was allowed to see and feel. It was in my late twenties, some years before my experience with Mr Fricker that I was on my knees in prayer position asking for confirmation from Him as to what he looked like. It seemed there were so many interpretations, yet nothing I could visualise clearly. This experience was my confirmation. Even now, when things get a bit weary I remind myself of that special moment. Throughout my life in times of stress or need, I have always prayed and talked to the higher being, not knowing who it was but understanding there was something bigger than us.

Mr Fricker offered me one piece of wisdom as I was leaving his office after a particular visit. In my mind, understanding what he was able to do for me I wanted to share that with the world and especially the ones I loved. It was at this point that he explained that everyone is on their own path and some people, regardless of their situation need to experience the difficulties of life and healing of that will come for everyone at different times and in different ways.

I went about life and enjoyed being a mother; watching my children grow and develop their personalities. I loved them both equally. Even though each were totally different, they were a great inspiration to me. Watching them grow each day, month and passing year. I occasionally even dressed them in identical clothes, being only three years apart as anyone with two daughters close together will know when you buy one thing you nearly always make sure they both have the same. Treating them equally was always very important to me.

As each one of us walks through life, we all have a different journey and life lessons to work through. These lessons are not likely the same from person to person and even with my own children, I could see they are here with different paths ahead of them. The lessons shall be learnt and after each trial it's important to reflect on what has been learnt, make the necessary changes and continue ahead closing that chapter on what is now understood and moving onto the next.I am told there are about 4,000 traits known to us as human beings and to recognize this in one another, is an important part of our souls growth. Annoyances of that in another person can often reflect traits in yourself you are yet to acknowledge. We are all part of the whole and none of us are any better or any worse than another. We are equal in the game of life and all form a part of the source, which is divine love. Loving and accepting people for who they are, and learning to understand why we behave in certain ways at certain times, and to know it is alright. Remember that your creator loves you unconditionally whoever you perceive them to be.

Reading this book so far, you will realize that my first husband hasn't been mentioned often.

# First Husband

As time went on my husband and I had less and less in common. There was very little conversation between us which meant communication was extremely poor. He was also quite moody at times and eventually he would come home from work, have a meal, get bathed and read his paper and unfortunately never interacting with his children. I became well aware as to what was happening, but each time I tried to talk to him, he would walk out the house.

As I was unable to hold a conversation I knew that eventually things would come to an end, because in a relationship you have to be able to talk to one another and mostly listen to what the other person has to say and validate one another's feelings. That way you can always work something out. But unfortunately this never happened. I did think of leaving with the children, but in those days it wasn't easy. Where was I to go with two small children? I was also working in a betting office, but not earning enough for us to live off, and didn't know about social security at that time. My eldest daughter saw more than I wanted her too and we tried to keep it from Jane, but realized looking back now that she did pick up on certain things. The only time he did want to talk to me was to get me to sign over a large amount of money that was capital on the home. Knowing how things were in my heart I knew I should have said no, however still playing the supportive wife wanted to assist his desire for success. As time went by it didn't matter anyway it became impossible on both our parts. My energy levels depleted and although I was carrying through the motions of each day, inside I felt as though I was dying. I wasn't living my truth.

Angel Experience: Although I felt the way I did, I was still married and going through the motions of my life. I went to the local shops and looking in a man's clothing store near were we lived, I saw some beautiful shirts and thinking quietly to myself there was no point, he really didn't care either way. 'when at that precise moment a tall man who looked in fifties and well-built was stood beside me and simply said "'a little of your own is better than a lot of someone elses", then when I turned to look at him again he seemed to have disappeared. Those words from a stranger left an impression on me and suddenly I felt safe no matter what the future brought.

It was whilst all of this was going on that tragedy struck. My beloved youngest brother Graham who was a Master Baker with a physique to match had a fatal accident. He was out celebrating his engagement on the 17th July 1983. I will remember the date well. As when I asked him why he chose that day and not his birthday which was July 2nd he couldn't answer. I believe this was a date deep in his subconscious although I could be wrong. This event was soul destroying I couldn't believe what was happening. *Previous to the time of my brother becoming engaged, at his request, we visited a Clairvoyant together and when we came out he turned to me and said how come you were given dates and I wasn't?. Which was to come to light later. He also told me a year before his fatal accident that he had a dream about our Nanna and Grandad, which was unusual because he didn't know them that well.'He dreamt that they came and showed him around on the other side, and as they had already passed over, all he could remembered was that they said you must go back now.!When he told me this I felt fear, but tried not to think too much about it, after all he was looking forward to a future with his girlfriend and they were looking at houses together because they would eventually get married.*

I remember visiting mum and dads on the Friday before the accident it was a beautiful sunny day, I was on my way to work and mum and dad were at the front gate talking. I asked them where Graham was and dad told me he was still sleeping after his nightshift and asked if I wanted to wake him up as he would be going to work soon. I went upstairs and I remember him just rousing and I started to talk to him about a house he was interested in buying with his future wife. There he was laid there with his hands behind his head talking about his future. Little did I realize that that was to be the last time we spoke on this earthly plane.

The call came about 11 pm on the following Sunday night and was told that Graham had been involved in an accident and had been flown to the nearest hospital with a Neuro Surgeon. By the time we arrived the Neuro Surgeon was operating on him. All the family was there through the night including his fiancé. Our emotions were all over the place you want to be angry with him, telling him off for being so silly all while praying he would pull through.

My first husband and I drove home that night and came back early in the morning, whilst my brother Pete sat with our younger brother Graham most of the night. My mother, father and Grahams fiancé were close by should anything happen.

The next morning on our way back to the hospital, I kept thinking that I hoped my dad doesn't have to make the decision to switch off the life support, as it would have destroyed him. As previously outlined my father delivered my baby brother into the world and the thought that he would have to make that final decision to take him out of it, would be too-much to take.

All that day I would catch glimpses at my dad standing behind my mother, I couldn't look at him for long as the pain in his eyes was too-much to bear. He was trying to be strong for my mother's sake, but I could feel his pain and to this day, will never forget that haunted look on his face. My first husband got a lift back home with someone as he had to go back to work, so I had a car spare to take others home if needed.

I went in to see my baby brother with whom I used to feed regularly and take him on walks in his pram, and looked after him whenever needed, even occasionally bathing him the sink. As I stood at the side of the bed on my own listening to the beeping of the machine his face looked quiet rosy. I started to will him to get better with every bit of my heart and soul. Then when the nurse came in to monitor his progress on the machine, she actually went away and brought the doctor back. It was then something Graham had said to me once, when we went out shopping together, that came to mind. He had a friend who had been involved in an accident that left him severely disabled and with a poor quality of life, Graham made it very clear he would never want to be in that position. It was in that moment that I thought to myself that I had no right to will him to live if that was to be the result. With that thought I let go and let God take over.

The Surgeon came into the room where we were all sitting and made the final decision to switch the life support machine off. I felt relief that dad didn't have to make that decision. I have no idea how I managed to then drive his fiancé and two other people home the 50 miles it took to get there, all I remember is my eyes were directly staring straight ahead all the way to Graham's fiancé's house. Everyone stepped out of the car and people were talking to me and I couldn't respond, I couldn't even talk, eventually someone helped me out the car and sat me down in the house. It was only when someone placed a neat Brandy in my hands and lifted it up to my mouth that I started to come around, likely in a catatonic state.

From then on, I would occasionally for the weeks after wake up in a mornings and have to feel my limbs as it felt like a part of me was missing. We all stuck together as families do and took it in turns to stay with mum and dad for a little while. On one occasion the vicar came to see them and to talk with my parents, understandably my mother was very angry at this stage, refusing to believe a god would have taken her child away. She had lost her faith. Even in those times I still believed there was a reason for what had happened even if I didn't understand it it's as though your life has stood still and everyone around you is moving.

He was loved by so many people cars lined the whole street, the church was full and it took two cars to carry the mountain of wreaths. This beautiful boy was no longer in this physical world and I will be forever grateful that I got to see him a few days before the accident on that Sunday. Our father actually told us that before he went out that fatal night, he had tidied his bedroom, which was something he was constantly asking him to do. Not long after his passing, I was approached by my nephew Greg to say a friend of his was asking to see me. His friends name was Phil and he was to clairvoyant who had indicated to Greg that I would understand his request., I went along with Greg to see Phil who proceeded to tell me that Graham had died before his time and would be re-borne back into the family to finish his Sacred Contract and that I would know who it was.

# Ending Of a Marriage

*T*he week we buried my brother Greg I was being strong for mum and dad, at thirty seven years old now I now feel I am getting wiser and stronger and held my own emotions in until I got home. Then once the children were in bed, I would pour a glass of brandy, sit alone and allow myself to grieve.

Things by this stage were really not good between my husband and I, however all continued on the way they were for another year. During this time I suspected he was being unfaithful and knew he no longer wanted to be with me, while I felt the same. As always, our intuition is very rarely incorrect. I had many signs that he was indeed having an affair yet brushed over most of them through either naivety or denial, it could really have been either. Once getting dropped off from a night out by a female and then finding a letter in the back of the car written to him by another woman thanking him for their time together, believe it or not he even had an answer for this. Of course it wasn't his letter and he didn't know why it was there. And I chose to leave it there, I was young and somewhat vulnerable without the energy to fight.

I was once told by a clairvoyant "Never believe what is told you and only half believe what you see", sage words which turned out to be true.

Over time I had lost my identity. During our 17 year marriage I felt I had become a shadow of my former self and almost became institutionalised within it. My former friend who lived next door to me came back into my life and I used this as an opportunity to open up to her about what was going on. She was also married yet I believe that was also coming to an end as he had met someone else. I introduced her to my husband and brought her into our lives, again confiding in her what was happening between us.

It was the month of August in the following year that things finally came to a head. My suspicions were confirmed that he was indeed having an affair, with no other than the girl who grew up living next to me. Of course he denied this at the time, but as with most things the truth always comes out in the end.

Sadly things were past a point of recovery, his way of dealing with this was to put me down rather than having an open conversation about where things were at. One positive arose throughout this negative experience in that I learnt was to nurture myself. A nice hot bath and the occasional glass of brandy generally did the trick. One night when I was feeling particularly low, I poured myself a brandy and lemonade and took it to bed, he came home in his usual state of mind and things erupted. By this point I really had had enough and while the argument ensued Graham my late brother flashed through my mind and all I could think of was, how hurt he would be if he could see what was happening.

This was my turning point and Graham gave me the courage to be strong and to respect myself moving forward and although I wasn't sure of what the future would hold, I knew that separating from my husband was the best decision. This turned out to be the night the end of our marriage would be cemented. He left and returned the next day to collect his things and I felt emotionless over the whole situation, I had reached my capacity to fight for it and was ready to let it go. After he had left, I remember walking out into the front garden where the roses were blooming and everything seemed brighter. The colours were stronger, the grass greener and the sky bluer like a cloud had just lifted and I knew in that moment it was the right thing. From this point on my children and their feelings were what mattered the most. Taking each day as it came was the only thing I could do, it is impossible to know what the future holds but putting one foot in front of the other is the first step. Everything always works out how it should, we are taken care of on a higher level and it's most important to follow your heart and have faith, however rough the road may look.

As the saying goes YESTERDAYS HISTORY, TOMORROWS A MYSTERY, THE GIFT IS THE PRESENT, THE PRESENT IS THE GIFT.I look back at my life now and wouldn't have had it any other way. I feel I have grown so much and have come to realize that in the grand scheme of things whatever happens to us as individuals, we will always be taken care of and what happens to us will always be for our highest will and good. When we signed our Sacred Contracts all of our trials were discussed and the people who are in our lives for an hour, a day a month and year or a lifetime, come in for a reason. Each individual we meet we learn something from and also they too in return learn something from ourselves. It is the way it has been written, so trust in the bigger picture and let it take the shape in the way it's supposed to.

# Visit From The Otherside

The following Christmas of the same year after my ex had left in the August we spent Christmas at my parents' house. It was Christmas day and the girls Amanda, Jane and myself had a delicious family meal together, all full from lunch we all sat down to watch the television I was beginning to feel a little sleepy. On my dads suggestion I took myself upstairs to have a rest in the spare bedroom, the one that I had last spoke to my brother in before he died. Getting snuggled up in bed I began dozing off and found myself in that lovely state somewhere between sleep and consciousness. I felt a cold draft on my back as though someone had lifted the bed sheets but in my sleepy state accepted it was one of the girls. The same draft hit my back as I began to awake and my first thoughts it was one of my daughters checking on me. When I eventually awoke and went downstairs. I firstly asked who had been checking on me?

They all looked blankly at me and explained no-one had been upstairs during that time, not once. Dad looked towards me and asked whether the door was shut when I went to sleep and whether it was again when I awoke, I realized in that moment what he was thinking and I agreed. I believe it was my brother who had paid me a visit.

During this time my sister-in-law Stephanie was diagnosed and dying from cancer. Stephanie was my older brother Mark's wife and understandably Mark was struggling with the situation and started to do some soul searching. He requested that my mum and dad accompany him to a spiritual church thinking this may offer him some understanding of where life was headed. They agreed and went along. He was randomly selected and a lady, with a hand on his shoulder indicated she was seeing a daffodil associated with him. While I didn't attend the church my dad afterwards told me what had happened, Mark didn't understand the correlation however both dad and myself thought it could be pointing to her passing in the spring. Of course, we didn't tell this to him as we may have been wrong. Sadly though, we were not.

It was during this time before her passing that I experienced my first and last experience with communicating through my dreams, that I am aware of. I recall the conversation word for word. I had had a brief encounter only weeks before but upon hearing my late brothers voice sat straight up in bed, wide awake. This time however my vision was different. I was dreaming of watching children playing on the mound of soil and grass that was in our garden they were laughing and having lots of fun. When from the back of my head I heard my brother Grahams laughter and as I was about to wake, I heard him stress to me DON'T WAKE UP!! DON'T WAKE UP!!DON'T.... WAKE ....UP!!

I must have relaxed at that point, as we entered into a conversation. I asked him how he was, he told me he was busy over there. The exact words were "I am busy here you know, I have my work to do". I then started asking questions about the family on earth and if they would be alright. All was well with everyone until I asked about my sister-in-law Stephanie, as of course we all live in hope but it was at this point that everything went silent and I have never heard from him since. That morning when I awoke I knew and felt that I had been privileged to receive such an experience and its a feeling to this day I will always remember.

It was not long after this that I met my third daughters father around the October time, and seven months later my dear sister-in-law passed over, in the month of May. I was three months pregnant.

# Daughter's Growing Up

*C*arrier bag incident.

Life continued and my daughters were growing up fast Amanda had recently started a part-time job working in a retail shop at the local shopping centre and this is where she was to meet her future husband, who was the manager. One day, when I had returned home from work Amanda was talking away to Will on the phone when he said he wanted to speak to me. At this point I had never met him so I agreed and said "Hello". The conversation went something like this 'Hello my name is Will, you will like me!". I was shocked and felt the hairs on the back of my neck stand up. I replied "Will I?" Of course Amanda was my first born and in my own questionable experiences to this point I wanted to make sure she was safe and wondered to myself how I might be able to bring him down a peg or two? He was being very presumptuous. The next day Amanda came home with something she had bought from the shop where she worked, which was in a carrier bag with the name of the shop written on it. It was then I had an idea, a lightbulb moment you might say. The next day while I was still in that frame of mind I donned my stylish faux fur coat with slits up each side, long boots, did my hair and makeup and ensured I looked the part of the sophisticated woman I was going for, and off I went to return his empty carrier bag. Once I arrived at the store I spoke to a young girl behind the counter and asked to speak with her manager. The assistant looked at what she thought was a returned item in the carrier bag and asked to help.

I politely declined and explained I would like to speak personally with the manager. Again, glancing down at the carrier bag she then went upstairs to bring him down, but he was some time, so I continued to look around the shop with poise and grace. Eventually when he made it down to the shop floor, Will (not knowing who I was) arrived with an annoyed look on his face and asked how he could help me. My reply, while not one I had rehearsed had the exact effect I was hoping for, taking a breath I said "I am Amanda's mother". It was fun to watch him do a complete 360 degree turn, not metaphorically, but literally. On the spot right there in front of me.

I then smiled and left the shop; later on I learned that he said he wished the ground had swallowed him up at that time. I believe it brought that over confident young man down a peg or two, don't you?

Amanda and Will eventually married and moved away from our home town. For a couple of years it was difficult for us to travel to where they were living as I didn't have a car, so only managed to visit once with my brother Pete driving. Fortunately after a couple of years, they then they moved to an area which was easier for me to travel to and closer to her home town. One Christmas in particular I took Jane who was 16yrs old and Kate who was just over 2yrs old at the time to where their eldest sister lived, which then has only an hours journey on the train. We spent Christmas at Amanda's and Will's where we had a lovely time before returning home on the train. walking home from the train station, it was a cold, dark December night. As we walked the empty streets home, pushing Kate in her pram I told Jane that when we get home we could all get in the same bed and eat lots of chocolate, and we did just that. A perfect finish to the festive season.

## Kates Father

To be honest it wasn't long after the visitation from my beloved brother Graham, that I met Kate's father Matt. I had seen him lots of times before when he came into the place I was working; he was tall, slim and Scandinavian looking. It was when

Matt noticed I wasn't wearing a wedding ring that we got chatting, as we never spoke much before. It was only days later that he sent me a huge bouquet of flowers and after what I had been through with my ex-husband, I enjoyed the attention.

We then began seeing each other and went out on dates wining, dining and talking until the early hours of the morning. On one very strange occasion my ex-husband rang the home number the next day to say that he knew that I had someone in the house! I did recall hearing someone the night before in the front garden, but paid little attention to it. I'm not sure what his aim was of this, but to be honest I didn't care, he had chosen to leave. Bryan had tried so hard to make me look the guilty partner through the divorce, even hiring a detective. I know this as I would see the same man driving past the house on multiple occasions, staring straight in through the front window which was all so ridiculous to me. One of the final promises he made me was that he would 'see me in the gutter first', If only he realized I didn't care about any of the material things he did.

Back to Matt, our relationship progressed and I met his family, but what I couldn't understand was that every time I met different members they would say "you better look after this one". I always found it odd and for it to be continually uttered, I wondered the meaning behind it. I eventually was to find out at a later date.

Eventually we ended up in bed together, and one day when Matt got out of bed and made his way downstairs he fell. I heard the thud and crash as he skittled to the bottom and I jumped out to make sure he was ok. Lying prostrate at the bottom of the stairs he told me he believed he had been pushed! (My beloved brother Graham who had passed flashed through my mind, but I never passed comment). As time went by I was indeed pregnant, but not at that particular time,. I found out sometime the following March that Kate was due in the November, a Scorpio as was my sister-in-law who had passed, Stephanie. On the night Kate was born, it was cold and dark and the first snow of winter had begun. It was around 11.30pm when we decided to go to the maternity home as my labour pains were strong. When we arrived and because we hadn't rung ahead all doors of the maternity home were all locked. I remember thinking to myself that this looked like something out of Fawlty Towers because Matt being tall and lanky, was running around pulling at all the doors and shouting "We're having a baby!" My eldest daughter Amanda was with us all the way and when I was in the delivery room and about to give birth, I took one look at her face and could see that she was getting quite anxious, I asked if she would like to leave and with a quick nod, she left. A couple of minutes later Kate came into the world and as the nurse put her in the crib, she simply said "You can tell she's been her before!"

Kate's eyes were open and her head moving around and it was then that Amanda popped her head around the door and asked if it was over and safe for her to come in. From the day Kate was born, you could almost see her personality. When Kate's father came to visit he would talk constantly to Kate about anything and everything, giving her plenty of mental stimulation. But it wasn't long before I started to see the other side of Kate's father, he would disappear for days on end and money sometimes went astray. I had taken maternity leave and would be going back to work about following March. If I think about it, I wasn't that bothered that Matt would go missing and turn up out of the blue as I had Kate. A precious memory that will always be with me was when I would be giving her a bottle, we would be staring into one another's eyes and Kate would suddenly give me a big grin, I would grin back and then she would start laughing and that laugh would make me laugh and so it went on for a good few minutes.

# Kate's Father a Realisation

$\mathcal{A}$s my relationship with Matt continued to deteriorate one particular time that really hurt was whilst I was feeding Kate, her father came in looking for an argument and as I wasn't listening because I was engrossed in feeding Kate, he took her out of my arms in the middle of her feed and started her crying and even when I asked he refused to give her to me. This was the start that led to other things of how he would treat me, when his mother came he ordered me about telling me what to do. I couldn't go out the house for long without him wanting to know where I had been and dare not be long when I did go out and I knew this was not a good place to be. I was once changing Kate's nappy in front of the television when he became very aggressive as I was blocking the view of the football. Without going into the details, this was a turning point for me and I knew it had to end and that Kate and I would be better off without him in our lives. Going to work the next day, I had a bruise on the side of my lip that was noticed by my colleagues which only affirmed for me that I needed to move out. That night after work I went to mum and dad's to pick Kate up I knew she was safe there. When I arrived I told them I was leaving Kate's father, and that's when my dad said something very important to me. It was "If you're going to do it, do it now because knowing you, you will change your mind in the morning". Turns out dad knew me better than I knew myself.

With those thoughts I went home. Matt's mother was standing in the kitchen when I arrived and he was laid out in front of the fire recovering from a hangover. I told his mother before speaking with him and her response was that I should tell him now. I stood in the doorway with my knees shaking so much I thought they would give way and told him I was leaving. He said "Well you're not taking Kate" and my answer to that was, he knew I would never leave without her. With that he stood up, brushed passed me and walked out the door, ironically driving off in my car. His mother warned me that if I was going, then to do it before he returned.

I rang my dad who got his friend Charlie from across the road to come and pick us up, I took the cot and anything else I could gather, leaving the mortgage money in a tin and my jewellery which I later asked my eldest daughter Amanda to get when she went back for her things.

# Staying at Mum and Dad's

$\mathcal{W}$ e stayed at my Mum & Dad's whilst I figured out the next move, along with my eldest daughter Amanda who was seventeen years old at the time. Amanda made it clear that if I intended to return to Matt that she wouldn't be coming with me. I think at that time it gave me the added strength to stick to my guns and keep moving forward. Jane, my middle daughter had already left and chosen to live with her father when Matt arrived on the scene, looking back she must have had some insight into his character that I couldn't see at the time. Without understanding any legal parameters or what I would be entitled to, I went to see a solicitor. Taking Kate with me, I can visualize myself sitting with my six month old daughter in my arms not knowing what I could expect or where this new chapter might take me, whilst waiting to be called in.

When my time came, I explained my situation to the solicitor he asked me if I wanted him out and to move back in? I must have looked dumb because I said I wouldn't mind as I had no real intention for the future. He then drew up a court order to get him out of the house and a restraining order stop him coming near me or returning to the house.

I knew when he had received the papers because he came barging in to where I worked. I remember just standing there and not speaking a word, as I wasn't going to antagonize the situation. Once the way was clear, we moved back in.

Upon our return to the house my lawn mower and the washing machine were both broken and any money that had been there for the mortgage or from Kates pouch had gone. I remember sitting my daughter in her low chair in the middle of the lounge and being on my knees beside her, the television was working so I switched it on and with that the song Amazing Grace came on. The tears just flowed and flowed as that song said it all, it was me. Looking at my daughter I said "Well my darling it's you and me against the world".

# *Visits for Kate*

$I$t was around two months after going back home with my daughters Amanda and Kate that Amanda came to tell me she too was moving away with her boyfriend, Will. He had been transferred to another part of the country with the company he worked for and she was going with him. I knew this was coming, but didn't realize how hurt and upset I would be. I burst into tears and they just flowed like someone had turned on a tap that wouldn't stop. I was devastated, but understood it wasn't about me, it was about what my daughter wanted and as long as she was happy that was all that mattered.

Once Amanda had moved out, Kate and I got on with our life and by this time she was around nine months old. Whilst I had returned to work part time when she was six months it was becoming difficult with all the traveling involved and no car. It was inevitable at that stage that I had to give up work and focus on my daughter, getting my priorities right as it were.

While it was a struggle financially at first, my priority was always to pay the mortgage and the rates. That way I secured a roof over our heads. It was my thought that if I couldn't pay the others I could improvise with candles etc. This of course was the worst case scenario and fortunately I was able to organize myself before it ever got to that point, the important thing to remember was to keep paying the mortgage and to keep that roof over our heads. I would pay the utility bills each week in stamps, and whatever money left over would be for food.

Looking back that time was my biggest challenge. I remember having to go on government benefits which is something I had never heard of until then. As I looked around me at the local office I observed many desperate people, itching to get their next pay cheque. One man, around twenty three years old laid across a seat and seemed not to care one way or the other as long as he got some money. Another lady was shouting at the assistant behind the counter who was simply trying to do her job. Listening to this verbal abuse it was in that moment I realized just how terrible life can be if you let it get to you and that personally this was where I had reached rock bottom. The best thing about hitting rock bottom? The only way is up! A song by Black Box which became my affirmatiom. When I saw the lady at the counter and explained the situation, she was very helpful. She asked whether I wanted to pursue the child support I was owed, however seeing the situation as it was I was concerned this would open up a can of worms that I didn't need. I was entering a world I knew very little about and was learning fast.

Soon enough I gained a routine and each day I would rise and get organized. Firstly would get Kate up, prepare breakfast, put her in her pram in the back garden while I cleaned the house and then finally we would go out for a walk. On nice warm sunny days, I loved taking her out in her pram, I would buy a newspaper and head to the rose gardens in the nearby park to sit on a bench with Kate sleeping in her pram next to me whilst I was reading the paper; it was very peaceful. To be honest what I had been through in the past, I appreciated being in the moment all the more. This was a ritual that went on for a long time and as Kate got older she would get up and ask where we were going today mum?

If you're a single mum with a small child, it would be my advice to take yourself and child out each day, even if just for just an hour it helps both of you to feel better and is a win-win situation.

In the beginning Kate's father would take her out on certain days, but it wasn't long before he started to let her down. I would get Kate ready on numerous occasions and she would stand at the window, ready with her coat on and best shoes, waiting excitedly for her father to pick her up. She would wait and wait until eventually I had to tell her it will be another day. He did this too-many times and I decided enough was enough. I pulled the plug so to speak as I couldn't stand to see her little face so sad and knew if this continued it would lead to a very insecure child, so made a conscious decision to tell him he was no longer welcome until she was old enough to better understand the situation. To me, it was almost a welcomed relief. There was always an unease in me whenever he would leave with Kate and whether that seems selfish or protective is for you to decide. That said, I never spoke a bad word about him to Kate as that was only wasted energy and as with everything the truth always comes out in the end. One particularly special moment I'd like to note was when Kate was around two years old. She was on her little three wheeler tricycle and as she was squeezing past me in the kitchen she said "Scusie mamma" in a strong Italian accent. I thought it must have been from a past life as I had no idea where she would have heard such a phrase from, let alone accent.

# Jane Returning Home

As time went by and Kate's first birthday approached, I contacted the solicitors to tell him my intentions to get in touch with my middle daughter Jane while at school. I mentioned earlier that when Matt came onto the scene, Jane had moved home with her father, which unfortunately wasn't under the best circumstances. Jane was upset with me for having Matt in my life and wouldn't speak with me from that point on. I tried to contact her daily at her father's home, however was consistently told she wasn't there. It had been over a year when I decided enough was enough. The solicitor made a phone call to the Headmaster of the school that Jane attended, and through the correct channels I got permission to see her.

The meeting was organized and under the supervision of the headmaster I finally got to see my daughter. It was very emotional and there were tears all round. I told Jane that Matt was no longer in our lives and welcomed her back home, whenever or if ever she wanted to come. When I looked up at her all I could see was eyeliner and mascara running down her face, I loved her so much and more than I think she would ever know. The head teacher or principal gave us both tissues and I started to wipe her eyes. To my joy from the day of the meeting Jane decided to come back home and my life was complete again. I'll never forget seeing her turn up in a taxi with a teddy bear in her arms for Kate which was moving..

Luckily for me

I also managed to attend night school whilst Jane was home. I took a course in Sociology and emotionally the time apart was good for both myself and Kate. Jane also arranged a surprise birthday party for my fortieth, which really was a surprise as I had no idea. She had gone to great lengths and there were so many people there when I walked in the door, seeing the family and friends there, really meant a lot to me.

# Divorce Settlement

*I*t was to be two years later that my the divorce settlement from my ex-husband was finally coming to an end. It had been an emotionally draining experience, receiving odd letters from solicitors asking me to explain what had happened to certain pieces of jewelry or other items which my response was always the same, that it was sold to pay bills. Divorce is difficult whether you are happy to be separated or not. Receiving these letters is commonplace and my one piece of advice to anyone going through the same experience would be to read it, put the paper down and consider it tomorrow. Things are always clearer after a nights sleep. With Matt out picture and the final settlement of my divorce, I was beginning to feel as though things were coming together. Jane and Kate were my reasons for getting up in a morning seeing their happy smiling faces, I knew it was my job to keep a roof over our heads and be mother and father to Jane and Kate. What did amaze me was that as young as Kate was, and the age difference was some fourteen-years, between her and her sister, she could hold her own if they were disagreeing. A few years later Jane met someone and they moved into their own home together. I got on with my life raising my youngest daughter on my own and you know what!, I was happy. Of course I had my worries like everyone at times, sometimes over paying bills and a mortgage but that taught me to live one day at a time. With the support of my parents and my dearest friend Liz between them they would look after Kate, while I went on a retraining program learning to use a word processor three days a week, it was fairly new back then in 1989, but I really enjoyed it.

It wasn't long before I was offered a full time job in mortgages and finance at a company in the center of town. I found a child minder to look after Kate through word of mouth and on checking her credentials booked her in five days per week. She was also on the board of the school Kate would be going to later on and lived a stone's throw from the school gate.

To start with, my only transportation was a bike. I would take Kate to the child minders, leave my bike there and walk about a third of mile and catch the bus to my work. As Kate got bigger, I would have to ask her to sit really still with her knees almost touching her chin, because if she moved her head to look to one side, the bike would also lean. It really did take great skill!. I eventually acquired a company car to my great relief.

Life was good. I felt really strong and proud of myself, as things just kept on getting better and better. I had a good job, a nice car and was financially secure. The financial security was the one thing I talked to God or our Creator about. One New Year's Eve, I sat quietly and considered what it was now that I wanted to achieve and set to writing a letter to the powers that be of the things I wanted, while the details are now sketchy financial security was my number one. Comfort in not having to struggle between pay days and ultimately to find a partner who would love me for me and I could love in return. I would like everyone to consider that the higher power is always there to listen. Your requests never go unheard so ensure you always thank them for listening as it will always come to you, potentially not in the way you expect, but it will come. There were times when I would feel lonely of course, mainly at night when I would be switching off the lights but for me and at that moment in time, it was the best alternative. That was being realistic about life and having talks with myself for the reassurance of where I was headed. What I was to find out later was that my higher self was giving me the a pep talk, you see whilst we think we are at our loneliest we have in fact the most highest source always looking after us and are never really alone. What I have learnt is that in darkest hours something or someone will come along to lift our spirits. The same as when we get too full of ourselves or a bit cocky, something will generally happen to bring us back down – that is the balance in life that we all experience.

# Amanda's Wedding

*D*uring this time my eldest daughter Amanda was preparing to be married and her sisters Jane and Kate were both to be bridesmaids.

On the day everything went smoothly and Amanda and Will did their bridal waltz to Elvis Presley's, 'The Wonder of You'.

After the wedding my eldest daughter Amanda and her husband moved to the other side of London, around a four hours drive from our home town. In the years to come they had two children of their own David and Kylie, who have now grown into beautiful young people with personalities to match.

Time went on and changes happened within my work place. One of the directors was very straight forward and was really trying to make a go of the business partnership that had been formed, and the other partner seemed less invested and somewhat full of himself. On top of that he seemed to be a bit of a sweet talker, especially with the ladies. Information seemed to be getting hidden from me, and things started to appear as though they were cracking at the seams. It came to a head one day with a large fight between the directors within my ear shot and it was then that I could see the writing on the wall. Weeks later, the decision was taken from me. Arriving at work one morning the building had been cordoned off with police tape and I wasn't allowed in. The officer told me the questionable director had been arrested and I no longer worked there. One door closed.

After visiting the unemployment place, it wasn't long before I found myself another job working in a bakery just around the corner from where my daughter Kate and I lived. This worked out perfectly as Kate's school was only a ten minute walk away and meant she could walk from school and stay in the shop for the last hour before it was time to go home. When Kate had turned seven it was time for her first day of middle school after the long school holidays. Rushing around before work I hurried to get organised and get her to school on time. On arrival everything was quiet. Not a body to be seen with the main gates still locked. I had the dates wrong and was a week early! Well, we all make mistakes! I was lucky enough to have my mother and father not too far away and was able to drop Kate off there. I really had a great support team which I will be forever grateful for. My mother, and father and also my brother and his wife and of course my dear friend Liz. Due to their help, So I was able to keep working and it all worked out very well. While money wasn't abundant, Saturday I worked a half day and would ensure I dropped everyone cakes and perishables over that wouldn't keep for the next working day. It was my gesture of thanks that was important to me.

I worked mainly with Wendy at the shop, and she really was a very nice lady who had struggled to bring up her children on her own too. As by this stage I had a small car of my own, I would sometimes drive up to where she would be walking to work to offer her a lift. Wendy often seemed to put herself down. One day a gypsy came in our shop (as they were frequent in our town) and said I would be moving southwards (how far south became another story as it turned out to be Australia!) then she actioned with her hands that I was lucky as my spiral went up. Unfortunately Wendy's went down. The saddest thing was at this time Wendy was struggling with her menstrual flow, bleeding frequently which I asked her to see a doctor for on multiple occasions. For whatever reason, Wendy continued to delay seeing the doctor with differing excuses. After many months when she did decide to go it was much too late. During this time her daughter who was sixteen at the time became pregnant, Wendy eventually left work and her older sister who was a nurse took care of her until the end. I took a plant around to see her but her sister didn't let me in, so I would ring Wendy up on the phone. Eventually Wendy did return my call and was in immense pain, she was tired and no longer wanted to fight it. Wendy passed away soon after this.

This was another reminder of how precious and short life can be.

# Amazing Change of Jobs

$\mathcal{I}$ continued to work in the shop where I had with Wendy before her passing and one day after her daughter came into the shop to show me her new baby daughter. I peered in the pram to look at the baby I was astounded at how much she look like her grandmother that had died, the eyes were exactly the same, it was like looking into Wendy's eyes.

Eventually it became time for me to leave the bakery and look for another job and I ended up working as a doctors receptionist, it lasted about two months. Although I enjoyed it; the times weren't good for me to pick up Kate from school and it was time to look for something more suitable.

This led to telephone sales for a sports company, well needless to say all that talking either side of me became too much as you couldn't hear what the person on the other end of the phone was saying, so I ended up working back at the TAB this is when I met Kate's father. I was a jack of all trades you might say!

# Kate and I

When Kate was about four years old, she just loved playing outside with her friends in the street, sometimes we would be sat having a cuddle when one of her friends would knock on the door and she would go straight out, without a backward glance. I had to chase after her to ask her where she was going. She was always in a hurry to get wherever she was going and sometimes I would need to hold her until I felt her body relax. I didn't realize it then but I do understand that this is all a part of her personality. She is very outgoing, like a woman on a mission who wears her heart on her sleeve. She very open about the way she feels which can be a blessing, because you will always know where you stand and how she feels about you.

It always gave me great pleasure watching her as she grew, she had the confidence that I would have loved to have had. I often wondered if this is because she didn't have a dominant male role model while she was growing up. You see my younger brother Pete was her role model and he is a very patient and understanding person and someone who you could trust and rely on which I think rubbed off on her. To this day I will always have great respect for him.

# *Christmas Eve 1993*

*A* few years later on a Christmas Eve when Kate was about seven years old we went to see Amanda, her husband and the children who now lived the other side of London. The journey meant catching two trains. Firstly a train to London, then the underground train to the other side of London and then an overground train to where they lived. We were loaded up with presents and it was Christmas Eve and 6pm (not a good time to travel) when we caught the tube to Amanda's place. Cold and dark outside we sat down on the underground train. After hurrying to get on board with our bags and Christmas presents it wasn't until we were seated that I looked around and saw the weirdest looking people who seemed to be surrounding us. Three or four in total and they all seemed to be travelling separately, yet dressed similarly in black shabby looking clothing. At that moment I felt for the first time really frightened and vulnerable in the busy city. Looking back now I can only believe we must have been protected, because if ever there was a time for something bad to happen that would have been then. Thank you angels.

On a side note and only really as it has now come to mind while writing this, I think it is important to note that Kate seems to have an affinity with Italy. She once rang me while backpacking alone in her early twenties and walking in Venice and said "Mum, I have just had dejavu experience, I really feel I have been here before", even though it was her first time. This I can understand as there is a connection, that's my belief and I am sure also people reading this book experience dejavu with places or situations their physical body hasn't been before.

*Changes*

*I*t was August 1994 that a chance encounter was to eventually lead to the biggest change in my life to date, another significant sliding doors moment that only goes to reaffirm the truth in divine timing.

It was a regular sunny Sunday morning while I was vacuuming the lounge, that I received a phone call from my dear friend Liz. She had been at her local petrol station fuelling her car with her husband, when Mike came across and started speaking to her. Mike was a friend we had both gone to school with and had immigrated to Australia with his family when he was 19 years old. After exchanging the initial pleasantries Mike asked Liz some questions about me and my current situation. Whether I was married, had children and all of the regular life questions you might expect.

Mike indicated he would like to see me and Liz, without thinking, gave him my address. As those were the days before mobile phones were commonplace, Liz then rushed home to ring me and let me know he was on his way, it was in that moment I saw Mike and his friend walking towards my front door.

As a single mother living alone, I was always cautious in inviting people inside however made them both a coffee and kept them standing in the kitchen for an hour. It was lovely to catch up on all things over the last 30 years, his life in Australia and what I had been doing, reminiscing over the old school days and where everyone was now. As it came time for them to leave, Mike turned around, kissed me on the cheek and said "I'm coming back for you!"

It was around this time that my hip was gradually becoming worse. I was managing the pain as best I could through exercise and a malt vinegar rub that Mr Fricker had advised many years before. While this helped, it unfortunately got to the stage I had to take action and see someone. It was October 1994 and I was 47 years old when I made the appointment, the surgeon had reservations about operating on someone he deemed to be too young, however I assured him it wasn't the quantity, but the quality of life that mattered most. I was put on a waiting list to have an operation for a hip replacement. Luckily, the doctors surgery I visited had additional funding to use and I was able to have the operation in a private hospital the following March.

While nervous, I felt happy.

Things were jogging along nicely knowing that soon I would be given a new hip and a chance to start life afresh.

On February 14th 1995, a month before I was due to go in for my operation on March 13th, I received a valentine's card from Mike to say he would see me soon. Surprised, yet intrigued this led me to write a letter to him in response in case he arrived whilst I was in hospital. While I didn't have a return address for Mike in Australia, fate would have it that my daughter Jane, who was a hairdresser at the time, cut his sisters hair. I gave my letter to Jane to pass on and thought no more of things.

March 13th came, and I went to hospital for my operation. I busied myself the morning before going in, not allowing too much time to think of any potential consequences or the long recovery ahead and Jane came and picked me up in her yellow Volkswagon Beetle car to take me there. Checked in, the anaesthetist spoke with me and I was prepped for surgery early the next morning. It was while I was being wheeled in under sedation that I heard the surgeon querying to the nurse as to whether I might be a bleeder, I wanted to reply with yes however couldn't. While the surgery was over in the morning and I was taken back to my room, it wasn't until the following morning that I remember waking up. I felt at peace (potentially from the anaesthesia!) but also excited by the fact I had been handed a second chance at life and one that I didn't want to mess up. Two days seemed to go by in a blur while I was in and out of consciousness. I remember it must have been my birthday as one of my daughters was trying to show me cards and as much as I tried to keep my eyes open it just wasn't possible. My tubes were taken out and on the third day and I tried to get out of bed yet kept feeling dizzy. The nurse helped put me back into bed and they organised for another two units of blood. As I had celebrated my birthday whilst I was in hospital, I received a video that Amanda had sent. I opened the video with the nurses help, it was my two grandchildren David and Kylie who were two and five at the time singing happy birthday to me, needless to say I was overcome with emotion, it was very beautiful and heartfelt. After that the nurse would bring in another nurse to watch the video as word got around the hospital, it was really lovely.

# After My Hip Operation

$I$ was in hospital for ten days in total. My eldest daughter Amanda who lived four hours away rang to tell me she was coming down with her children to stay with me and make sure I was settled in. She was there the day after I returned home and cooked Kate and I enough food to last us two or three weeks, which was an absolute God send. It was lovely to see the grandchildren and offered a great comfort knowing they were there, I felt very loved and blessed and realised then that it was this love that holds us together. Its something money could never buy and that in itself was healing. Once Amanda had returned home, Kate although she was only 8yrs old looked after me in any way she could, making me cups of tea and preparing breakfast when possible before school. She would set me up with everything and prepare my breakfast and would bring it upstairs to me and if I needed a hand would help me to get dressed.

As time went on I had to learn to walk again, firstly with two sticks then after a week, one until eventually no sticks! It felt like a new lease on life once I was again mobile and pain free. I would walk for miles and miles, dragging Kate along for the ride, but luckily she also enjoyed it. Occasionally I would walk her too far that we would need to catch the bus back, but for me I just wanted to keep walking. I had never felt so free and revelled in every outing. I ensured I did the exercising outlined by the surgeon which to this day I still do religiously. There was no guarantee how long it would last so I vowed I would do everything I could to look after it, it's now been 20 years and it is still going strong!

# Mike

$\mathcal{I}$t was about late September when the phone rang and I received a call from Mike in Australia. He told me he was not happy in his marriage and while he had thought things might change, they never did., I don't know where it came from but my response was that he should come back to England. I guess in my mind I thought so we could see how things went, as after being alone with Kate for the last nine years I wasn't particularly looking for a partner or husband.

Over the next three months, we did a lot of talking on the phone. Mike would call and write me a letter every day before he arrived.

Mike always wanted to do the right thing by his family and I wouldn't have wanted it any other way. His children were all grown up, his youngest was eighteen in the following January and the two boys were older. Marriages are complicated and when children are involved they will generally always be your first priority. Mike would never have left the family while the children were younger and having being on the other side of the situation can understand the need to wait.

# New Chapter In Our Life Begins

$\mathcal{M}$ ike came to England on January 19th 1996. I remembered asking my brother and his wife, if they would be kind enough to have Kate stay whilst I travelled down to Heathrow to meet Mike off the plane. I was to stay with my eldest daughter Amanda the night before his flight arrived as she lived a 20 minute drive from the airport. Naturally everyone was concerned as to whether I was doing the right thing and must admit I was quite anxious also. As it happens it turned out the best move I had ever made,! We all have to take chances from time to time as this is how we experience life and the emotions that follow. After all, without emotions we wouldn't be alive!

I drove to the airport at 4am in the morning and arrived around 4.30am. Being that early it was quiet and the drive seemed smooth, everything actually seemed quite surreal. It was like I was travelling in a dream like state which is hard to describe but arrived with plenty of time ahead of his arrival. I walked around the airport for a while until a sign flashed on the screen that the flight had landed.

I made my move towards arrivals and watched at the barrier as people were coming through, I watched and waited, waited and watched and it was though everyone from the flight had already come through so naturally I started to worry as to what had happened, although I never had any doubt he would be there. Finally, I saw Mike walk through the gate. We smiled at each other and embraced at the arrivals gate, I remember us holding one another before we headed back to the car. It was time to begin our lives together.

We drove back to Amanda's house, Mike had a shower and changed before we started our journey back to our home town.

Mike wanted to drive the car so I let him and as it was a different car that he was used to, he was driving around 30mph under the speed limit. I thought this was quite funny at the time and something I wasn't used to, as cars sped past us. I kept this to myself though as this was better than him being the opposite way.

Stopping only once for a meal on our way back, we arrived home around 4pm. I arranged for Kate to stay with my brother for one extra day so we could continue this special time together.

# Back In Our Home Town

$\mathcal{A}$s we begin our journey together I had no idea of the changes that would occur in my life. Mike and I would talk for hours about everything, it was great to just listen to him speak.

We would take day trips around the country by just opening a map and closing our eyes and dropping a pin randomly around our region and that's where we would visit. The English countryside is so beautiful. As Mike had been away for so long he would love to just drive looking at the green pastures, hedgerows and trees and I was just happy to travel beside him. It wasn't just the country he missed, but the accent of our local town and I would love to watch him light up as he would hear people greet one another on the street.

It wasn't long however before Mike found a job, he was a hard worker and didn't like to be idle which was one of the many things I love about him. Off he would go each day, however it wasn't long before he realised the dog eat dog situation that it was for bricklayers in Britain. His first employer was for a man who he ended up nicknaming Robin Hood. 'Robin' would constantly short pay his employees, under paying them for number for bricks laid. What he didn't realise was Mike's vigilance however as he knew exactly how many he had laid. He would then be paid the missing amount the following week and so on and so forth. Mike was always prepared for the day ahead and on having an argument one day with some young guys who had taken advantage of his hard work, he walked off the job, not truly understanding the dire situation of the building industry in the UK. While work was plentyful for new builds in Australia, it was a very different situation in England. Ultimately, and reluctantly Mike had to return to work for the man he named Robin Hood.

I could see Mike wasn't happy with his working situation and things with his divorce still needed to be sorted back in Australia. He would ask me to return with him for only a couple of years so we could get ahead, but of course to leave my life and family at 49 years old seemed all too much. After much discussion, I finally agreed to return with him but only for a maximum of two years. That was all I was willing to commit to as even that felt a long time to be away.

We intended to be married while we were in Australia and I began to set the wheels in motion to apply for spousal residency and gain legal approval to take Kate out of the country, without her biological fathers consent. Luckily as he hadn't contributed financially or been a part of her life for the last 10 years this wasn't a problem.

Once the wheels were in motion, things moved quickly. Mike and I arranged to return to Australia shortly after Christmas to sort out the financial details of his divorce my dear brother and his wife would look after Kate whilst I was gone. We booked and paid for the tickets for the two of us, and off we went, expecting to be back within a month or two at the latest, however what took place after we left seemed to be a long series of events that extended this.

Flying from Manchester Airport, stopping in Dubai and then onto Melbourne I was somewhat concerned about the long haul flight as it was to be the first since having my hip replacement.

Luckily I didn't see this as an omen as it ended up being the longest of long haul flights! What should have been a 22 hour journey, ended up being four days in total. Delayed in both Dubai and landing in Melbourne due to ground fog and missing connecting flights it was something short of a nightmare. All in all though, we made it to Melbourne. Mike's daughter picked us up from the airport and dropped us off at a motel in the suburbs that night.

*Jane*

My daughter Jane left home in nineteen eighty eight, she was eighteen years old, to live with her boyfriend; all they had was an old house that needed a great deal of renovating and a mattress. It was what she wanted, she felt paying me lodge was better spent on her own house, which was probably the right thing for her at that time. They lived together for a good few years, about nine in fact. This didn't work out the way Jane had hoped. (*It was about this time that Mike came over from Australia and after a year talked me into going back with him for a couple of years*) She did keep the house, and it did get her moving on the property ladder so to speak. Jane was a hairdresser and has always had work and wasn't afraid of hard work.

She also did cuts at home and this is where she met her future husband Nick. They were both getting over a broken relationship and found they had a lot in common. It wasn't long before Nick moved in with her, and she fell pregnant with her daughter Vikki. (*I had already gone over to Australia by this time, I did manage to get back and spend time with them when Vikki was three weeks old*) They married when Vikki was about 2yrs and she was bridesmaid. When Vikki was 5yrs old she had a brother named Henry they adored one another and Nick was the perfect father, he did shift work which helped to fit in with Jane's hairdressing she was also working as a tutor at the college and as I was living in Australia was unable to help at that time although I did have my uses later on. It was fortunate also that Nick parents were also around to help whenever possible. Before I knew it I was flying back again, this is when 2yrs became 5yrs getting back every two years to England to see everyone. But eventually realising that as time went on I wouldn't be moving back to England in the immediate future. Both my daughters were distraught and dealt with it in different ways. The eldest one took to her step mum and tried to pretend that I was no longer in her life. Suddenly she stopped getting in touch and I was checking the post everyday but no contact at all. Until one day she rang me and told me how she had been feeling and how she had been trying to cope with me not being in the same country as her! *I now realise that at that time they were dealing with abandonment issues and that's not easy at all. As a mother I wish things could have been different, but my life now was with my husband in Australia. As the only good thing came out of my living in England were my beautiful daughters, unfortunately I did not have too many memories that were nice in England.* I believe that over time Jane resented the fact that I was so far away, which over time could have had an effect on her daughter Vikki. Remembering when I left Vikki, was nine years old, she was such a sweet adorable little girl; this is what I expected to see when I returned, but unfortunately this never happened, she was just thirteen and very hormonal.

# Arriving In Melbourne 1997

$I$ digressed once again. We arrived in Melbourne on a Thursday evening, Mike's daughter picked us up from the airport and dropped us at a motel.

Waking the next morning there was an awfully loud sound streaming in from outside and at first I wondered what it was. Soon I realised that this was the noise of constant traffic and I felt totally out of my comfort zone, it was all a bit overwhelming.

Without a plan, we eventually asked one of Mike's brothers if we could stay with them temporarily while we sorted our next steps. Living just outside of Melbourne, they agreed.

It was the summer time and the weather was averaging 40 degrees for the first few weeks of our arrival, something that being from England I was most definitely not accustomed to. That said, while everyone around me seemed to be stifling in the heat, I enjoyed every minute. It was almost as though my body had been deprived for so long of sun and warmth that I was drinking it in. Almost twenty years later however, it would now be a different story! While it was very kind of Mike's family to allow us to stay, it wasn't long before I started to become very homesick, longing for the place I had called home for the last 49 years. Understanding the situation it was then that Mike's brother suggested that we go away for a break to a place along the Murray River.

Using an old car borrowed from Mike's eldest son we arrived on what I would call a wing and a prayer! It was a five hour drive to our destination, a 40 degree day and with no air-conditioning it was a constant worry the car could break down at any minute with its constant coughing and spluttering. Not saying a word to one another Mike and I exchanged knowing glances of the situation we could be in should the worse occur, however we eventually made it – thank you angels!

While staying by the river, we began to make plans for our next steps. While it had been nice to stay with Mike's family we didn't want to overstay our welcome and needed our own space to regroup. We decided to check into a caravan park which was only a short bus ride from the beach and Mike found a temporary job to see us through.

Staying in the chalet I made the most of my time there, with little else to concern myself with in the short term I was able to really consider myself for the first time in a long time.

The chalet took very little cleaning and for the first time in my life I had seen wild budgerigars walking freely on the ground along with the other beautiful wild life such as Rainbow Lorikeets, Crimson Rosellas, and Galah's, it was truly a wonderful place. I would sit by the pool for an hour, then catch the bus into the nearby town and walk along the beach, sometimes taking my shoes off to have a paddle in the water and watch tiny school of fish swim in between my legs, *(even now I use this scene sometimes when I give a guided meditation, it really is quiet lovely).* Maybe then I would sit on the beach before going to have a coffee and do some food shopping before going back to the holiday park.

It wasn't long however that Mike's daughter came to stay with us at the holiday park and had nowhere to go as her and her mother didn't always see eye to eye. It was then things started to take another unexpected turn. We decided that rather trying to rent somewhere temporary, we could try to buy something for the two years we were here and sell it when we left, potentially making some money.

Luckily, Mike had a friend that worked at the bank and thanks to him we were quickly granted a loan and the house hunting began. It was our third inspection that we settled on a property and within a few short weeks we had moved in. Things seemed to be happening at such a speed that my feet weren't touching the floor.

We quickly got to work cleaning and painting the property as it was quite run down and I was due to return to the UK to collect Kate in just a few weeks. All the while holding faith that my proposed spousal visa would be approved as without this our dreams would come to an end.

# Trip Back To The UK The Same Year

*I* arrived back in the UK in March 1997, leaving Mike behind while I returned to settle the home and collect Kate. It was the first time I had travelled solo and while I was somewhat anxious, it was the only option. My eldest daughter Amanda and her ever welcoming smile, was there to meet me at the airport. Then eventually making my way back to my home town where my youngest daughter Kate had been staying with my younger brother and his lovely wife. My family has always been such a huge support in my life for which I am truly grateful for.

After this things seemed to happen really quickly. Returning to work, I happened to mention to a colleague that I needed someone to rent my house for the two years I planned to be away and straight away she said she was more than willing to rent off me. Once that was agreed, I received a call from immigration to say they didn't think we would make the intake for the end of April as there was a capping system that was close to its limit. Having said that only two days later I heard from them again to say I had got through and then the whirl-wind began.

The next three weeks were filled with cleaning, selling and storing furniture and visiting people for goodbyes. It was as though I was worried to stop or slow down for fear of changing my mind, so busied myself with what needed to be done, leaving no stone unturned. Before long the time arrived to leave and Kate and I were stood on the doorstep of the place we called home for the last 11years, bound for an adventure to the other side of the world. I will never forget the morning we departed from the station. Whilst waiting for the train the tide was in and the beach and sky looked beautiful, it felt almost as though it was saying goodbye to us. What followed was a 24 hour plane journey until we finally arrived in Melbourne. Kate was excited to see her new room that had been freshly painted before I left and the overall anticipation of being in a her new home, in a new country. Soon after, she was settled in her new primary school and only months after that she told me to not expect her to return to England as she was very happy with her new life. It was in this moment that my heart broke and I felt like someone had split me in half, it was a dreadful feeling. My intention was only ever to stay for two years. Mike and I married in the June of the same year and while it was only supposed to be very small with our two daughters and Mike's mother, the rest of Mike's family came in support which was very special. We of course would have loved to have invited them initially, but with very little money wanted to make it as affordable and low key as possible.

It was during that first year in Australia that my daughter Jane rang me to say she was expecting her first baby. Straight away I said I would be over, although not sure how we could afford it at that time I knew I had to be there, even if it meant developing a pair of wings to fly. I made it about three weeks after the baby was born and she was beautiful. Jane was a hairdresser and was catching up on clients that were wanting their hair cut, so soon after her daughter's birth. I could see it was getting too much for her and told her to leave it until she was feeling up to it. She was worried about her husband's reaction and what his expectations of her were, but after encouraging them to talk she was relieved and seemed more at peace after the conversation. Funnily, not long after Vikki was born Jane soon realised that the sound of the blow-dryer seemed to soothe her. Whether she was hairdressing or not, she would turn it on and Vikki would calm, likely a result of hearing it while in the womb.

I was to return to Australia, travelling from Jane's by coach to my eldest daughters Amanda's home (a *good eight hour journey by bus*) and spend some time with my other daughter and grandchildren before going back to Australia. It was Amanda that would take me to Heathrow

Airport where I would catch the plane back to Australia. It was a long trip but one I got used to over the years getting back to see my family and long term friends.

During my trips back and forth to England my father became very ill. It was just after Christmas in 1999, a few months after his 80th birthday in the July, I received a phone call from my mother who was very distressed about my father. He had to go into hospital and it wasn't sounding too good as he hadn't been well for a while. Being 12,000 miles away I felt so helpless and it was after hanging up the phone from my mother I decided to bring my flight time forward. Mike, Kate and myself were scheduled to fly over together in the June, however this felt too far away. Thankfully my dear husband was supportive of my going, even saying if I hadn't made the decision then he would have done it for me.I spent that time just being there for them and my children and grandchildren visited me whilst staying at my parents, even although sleeping on the settee was not good for my hip, so in the end everyone stepped in and I would alternate between staying with my daughter, brother and friends house and return to my parents home each morning to spend the day with them. Being there to do things that made dad happy was very important to me. Simple things like making him a salad or pancakes the things he enjoyed most, and his favourite chocolate mini rolls. My mother would be upset that he was hardly eating anything, but I explained to her that a little was better than nothing at all. It was heartbreaking to watch my mother struggle to help him. One particular time I remember her trying to carry a bowl of water into the bedroom for him to wash himself, but as she was so frail herself was really struggling. It took all of my strengh not to rush over and help her, but I believed my higher self was directing me to just let her do it. (In the past dad did the running about after mum).

Taking him to the hospital was very upsetting, especially as he had lost so much weight and they had trouble taking blood samples out of his arm which made it very painful for him. I was leaving the following Tuesday as dad went into hospital on the Wednesday and whilst waiting for the taxi to take me to the station, I knelt between the two chairs they were sitting on and held both their hands and not a word was spoken between us almost as if we knew it would be the last time we would all be together.j

Mike, Kate and I would be returning to England in June, as we had already booked and dad had given me the money so that I could return the same year so I knew I would be back.

I hadn't been back in Australia long, it was the Good Friday and Mike and I were out in the garden when the phone rang. It was my younger brother Pete and he was trying to tell me dad had passed over. Mike came bounding in his usual noisy self (*which is one of the many things as I love about him*) but on this particular occasion I just wanted quiet so I could absorb what my brother had just told me. Once he realised he went quiet, it would have been Thursday night over in England the year was 2000.

As I couldn't get back for his funeral about the time he was to be buried I went to our bedroom, and lit a candle and got into bed and went through the ceremony in my mind and allowed myself to grieve. Sometimes when I was down I would lay on the bed and even talked about my mother to dad even though he had passed... I would lay quietly and almost hear his words. I held guilt over not being there for my mother as of course my life had now been split between two countries.

We returned back to the UK in the June of the same year as planned, it was Kates first trip back since immigrating three years earlier. Kate visited her old friends and we set about seeing all of the family. When arriving at my mothers house, I walked straight in and sat in the chair my dad used to sit in to try and feel his presence. My mother was on bed rest after hurtng her back and after having my moment with my dad I made my way in to help her.

I intended to help my mother as much as I could and set about bed bathing her, cooking and assisting where I could. Spending time but also trying to share time because there were children and grandchildren friends and brothers and sister-in-laws to visit. My mother had a lot of help during this time, with people coming and going and get her in and out of bed which helped.

I was due to head back to Australia before Mike and Kate as my work as a primary school integration aide meant I needed to be back earlier.

We decided to have a little holiday in a caravan which we hadn't done before. While we enjoyed ourselves, the tension built up towards the end between Mike and my daughter, his step-daughter Kate. I became very distressed about the situation, and they decided to go out to the club whilst I did the packing. When they went I shed a few tears about all the upset and was worrying how they were getting on. At the end I finished the packing feeling a little down and in they walked as large as life as if nothing had happened! *(This is a Scorpio trait as they are both Scorpios).*

We travelled back to where we were staying with Mike's aunty and it was nearing the time for me to fly back to Australia. Two days before my return my mother had a bad fall and broke her hip. Which in turn started the downward spiral for her. This meant her being in hospital for some time and unfortunately the timing was terrible as I knew I needed to leave I had already had too much time off from my job. While she had lots of help from my brothers their wives and her grandchildren I knew she would resent my leaving, and when I visited to kiss her goodbye she turned the other cheek. Coupled with this, my middle daughter only told me she was due to be married after I had returned. With little time to discuss the hurt grew as I returned to Australia alone in that she did not want me there, if only she had spoken to me about it I would have at least tried to understand the situation. As it was obvious that it was too difficult with her father in attendance. Both my daughter Kate and Amanda would be there.

On Kate's return to Australia and as time went on I could tell she was holding in something and she became very upset over things my mother had said to her. On probing she explained that my mother often repeated that she didn't have a daughter (I was her only daughter) whenever Kate mentioned me around her. While this didn't surprise me, nor really upset me to be honest it was something Kate needed to discuss. She is very open and wears her heart on her sleeve so talking it through was helpful.

My younger brother and his wife, took excellent care of my mother after we had left for Australia and that put my mind at ease for as much as she denied I existed she was still my mother. They would take her shopping, do the cleaning and washing, they really were good and a blessing. I did ring my mother whilst she was in hospital and made my peace with her. I just would wish that she had the gift of understanding instead of being hurt like she was, because that's all it was. She was hurt that I wasn't there to look after her, but she wasn't on her own. Both her sons and grandchildren were there, whenever she needed them.

# First Teacher-aide Work

*W*e were now getting on with our life in Australia, which was for me to become one of spiritual growth.

Working as a teacher's aide for quite a few years with problem children, some of them proved to be very challenging at times. Travelling to school each day in the beginning made me feel quite sick in the stomach, so deep breathing was a ritual on my drive because no matter what these children had to know that they were cared for and loved and gaining their trust was paramount. Eventually they started to trust me as I played with them and made friends, gently guiding them to what was right and wrong.

My first child will always hold a special place in my heart. As an Aide it was my job and my job only to take care of the children and this particular child was initially quite tough to build trust with. As I was making progress an incident occurred that set us right back to the beginning. When waiting in line to enter the classroom a parent who was a volunteer approached and pulled my child out of line scolding her for a previous behaviour in front to everyone. I was shocked and upset at what to do so wrote a letter to the principle explaining what happened and that it should never happen again. From that moment on my little girl started to rebel all over again. I did eventually over time manage to get her back into my confidence. Her grandmother was caring for her and was getting all that was necessary help including seeing a psychiatrist on a regular basis. During the time I was working with her, we went out on a field trip where she would ask me to pretend to be her mother, which of course I said yes.

One day when she hurt her knee, I immediately took her to the sick room and tended the knee by cleaning it and putting a plaster on it. She looked up at me with her wide eyes and asked me if I was an angel. At the time I remember thinking this is the biggest accolade a child could give you! I replied that I was indeed her guardian Angel, words which just came out of my mouth without thinking.

She came to our home for dinner one day in December before school finished with written permission from her grandmother. We had a swimming pool back then and she was in and out of the pool for a long time, it was quite cold that day and it took us ages to get her out of the pool into the warm. When she finally did I gave her a towel to dry herself with, whilst I cooked some spaghetti bolognese. She came through to help and touched the pan, I winced and she looked up at me and said it's alright, and I said no it's not alright let me look at your hand. This child didn't value herself very much. This is when I told her that she was perfect just the way she is. And that when she grows up and meets a boy not settle for just anyone and to make sure he loved her just as she is. This little girl will always hold a special place in my heart.

# Second Job As A Teacher-aide

$I$t was here that I did my most growing and learning although we never really stop learning do we?

I was working nearer home this time and looking after a little boy who had Down Syndrome. His parents were of Indian origin and his mother had high expectations of him. One day I wouldn't let him do what he wanted and out of frustration he threatened to smash my car. That was because I was pushing him beyond his capabilities. He was a lovely boy about 11yrs old and it was to be his last year before he left for high school. As time went by I realised that it was life skills that he needed most. When we went out anywhere and had to buy food, he wasn't very confident and would want me to ask for him. So the next time we went out somewhere and had to buy food I encouraged him to do so. While he wasn't comfortable at first, he eventually did. We would repeat the same process of asking and paying each time and I believe this was a big achievement for him. He loved the computer and would get very frustrated with me if I tried to help, but could also be a big sweetheart as often children with Downs Syndrome are.

Occasionally I would also mind other children at the school when needed and it was during one of these times that I ran one through a meditation. While I had never really given it a name I realise I had been meditating for years. Sitting with one particular little girl in the sick bay who was waiting to be collected by her father, as unfortunately she suffered with seizures and I could see she was very frightened. I instinctively held the hand and asked her to close her eyes and took her through a meditation, although at that time I didn't realise it was. To me I was just trying to take her mind off things by letting her imagine she was in a field of beautiful flowers and a gentle breeze blowing in her hair, the sun shining down on her and we just let everything that was nice in the world be around us. This helped her to relax and feel safe.

There was an Autistic boy also that I looked after for a while, and one day he was being disruptive in the class, so I took him to the library. He chose a book and began to read to me and then I realised to my amazement that he wasn't actually looking at the words just the pictures. He was reading this book verbatim without even looking at one single word, not one word did he miss, but only kept looking at the pictures.

# Year 2000

$\mathcal{I}$n the year 2000 (*the same year my beloved father passed over*) I began my spiritual journey of the soul although I was unaware of most things at that time!

## Reiki/ Holistic Councelling

It was during my time as an Aide that I met another teachers- aide with whom I became good friends with. She would always be asking me to go to Reiki Practice with her, but I declined several times as I wasn't interested. I was at peace with myself and didn't feel the need. Married to a beautiful man, a lovely home, one of my daughters here with me and of course excellent health -, what more could I possibly want?. I had all that wanted and more besides along with the inner peace that I had craved for. Life was perfect. I often used an affirmation of 'inner peace' that I would project out to the deity I was channelling at that time, whether it be God, Jesus Christ, Angels or Goddesses our Creator who ever you percieve them to be I would speak from my heart and in my own way. *Ther is no set way in how you talk to light beings, whatever way you choose is the right way for you.* I was forever grateful for their guidance in seeing me through the darker times in my life. And to be where I now found myself was just phenomenal.

It was one day when watching the children play and my friend (*who was a teacher-aide*) began chatting to me and would regularly ask me to go to Reiki practice. I would always decline then she spoke to me about a meditation circle she attended at her healing centre. The thought seemed to sit right with me and I began attending on a regular basis. I enjoyed seeing people become more confident with themselves, myself included. They held different courses at the healing centre, and one brochure I picked up to look at and thought it could be interesting was a course on Holistic Counselling. However when I looked at all the electives it all seemed a bit much and I popped it back.

In the meantime I continued attending the healing meditation group.

Weeks went by and I decided to attend a numerology work shop, which I found very interesting, it gave us an insight into our life numbers and our characters. It was during this time a young lady came and sat next to me who was on the Holistic Counselling course downstairs. Her life number turned out to be the same as mine, which caught my interest and it was then she stood up and went over to a stand picked up a brochure and placed it in my hand. This was the same brochure I had picked up only a few weeks earlier.

And it was in the next moment that the lady who was running the numerology class turned around and said me I would be really good at it. It seemed almost symbolic as I had ignored the Holistic Counselling course at first and then to have the same brochure placed in my hands by another person was the confirmation I needed followed by the numerologist. Coincidence? I think not, as there is no such thing as coincidence.

When we were leaving I was walking downstairs and a small inner voice told me to do it now, if not you will change your mind tomorrow, so I enrolled before leaving the centre. The course was day class once a week over a period of twelve months and therefore didn't interfere with my job as a teacher's aide. It turned out to be a very self-healing journey and one I would recommend to anyone.

It wasn't until I looked at the brochure in depth that I noticed one of the electives was Reiki One.

These days 16 years on, whenever I teach Reiki (something I enjoy immensely)) I always say to my students that I came to do Reiki through the 'back door', as it was not my intention and I really wasn't interested at the time. (*Although realise now looking back on a subconscious level I must have been*).

# Mikao Usui System in Reiki

### Reiki One

### 2001

*O*n arriving at my first Reiki workshop, I was a little nervous at the unknown - going into uncharted waters as it were. My Reiki Master/ Teacher was a beautiful lady, tall with dark hair and with a soft voice. She had a very gentle energy about her. She worked closely with her husband who was an artist; he would paint the most beautiful images of energy and gods/goddesses, some of which looked very much like my teacher.

The workshop took place over two days usually a week apart to let the change of vibration within the body take place, which is discussed on the last day of Reiki One.

Day one was an in depth discussion about the history of Reiki and how it works. Running through a guide to the different hand positions and finally a Reiki practice sessions before embarking on the first part of your attunements to Reiki.

The second week moved into the discussion of the energy systems within the body and our chakras, learning that when imbalance occurs it can result in poor health then finally we start reiki practice followed by the second and final attunements for Reiki. It was on the last Saturday of Reiki One that I received my first angel experience although it took a couple of days later for the proverbial penny to drop. We were asked as a group at the end of our attunements if anyone had had an angel experience that they would like to share. I listened as some people spoke of their experiences, however I myself had nothing to share.

It wasn't until two days later my lightbulb moment occurred I went into my meditation room after taking the attunements, sitting quietly with my thoughts I began to go over the experiences of the last week. Thinking back to my first experience of receiving Reiki with my assigned partner and the Reiki master working on different parts of my body, I was focused only on my breath. My partner was working with her hands on my head the teacher with her hands on my feet. As my partner moved from my head to my solar plexus, located just above my naval I was aware the reiki master had taken her hands from my feet, it was then I felt a pair of hands placed on my knees somewhat larger than my teachers also feeling the heavy placement on my lower right leg I distinctly remember thinking her hands felt rather large but couldn't work out the heaviness against my leg which I can only decscribe as cloth like.

Of course as this was my first experience I did need to verify what I was remembering and after a phone call to the two people working on me at the time I was able to confirm my thoughts, I really had experienced my first Angel encounter, and it was very special. This was to be my first meeting of my Angel, who's name is Lydia. I am aware that when I meditate I feel her presence as a gentle hand placed on the right side of my shoulder blade.

As Angels are androgynous and don't have names you can ask for one through typing on your computer. Simply start by typing about the weather or any old thing comes to mind and all of a sudden a name will pop up out of the blue and voila, you have a name or your Angel. I have been blessed with many experiences since and so will you if you feel ready.

You see in our human state, we often fail to see the obvious. A wing against my leg, the hands that were larger than normal. What does it take for us humans to recognise that our angels are eternally with us and we only have to ask and say thank you for our needs or desires, trusting that it will be so. Be open and listen to that still small voice that comes from a loving place within. If it's not loving then dismiss it. Always ask them to help as they won't impose on your free will, and remember they just love to help. In my experience, after taking Reiki I, I knew straight away I would be taking Reiki Two.

At the end of each workshop you receive a certificate and a manual and your teacher is always available on the end of a phone should you wish to speak about any of your concerns.

During this time I was immersing myself in different courses for my spiritual growth. It was as though a candle had been lit inside my head and I wanted to keep learning all that was possible. From holistic counselling to numerology, crystals and meditation I was drinking it all in as at last I had found something that I really enjoyed doing, until then I really was jack of all trades and master of none doing many different types of work my journey continues. I am very thankful for my dear husband, who has always allowed me to spread my wings even though he didn't quite understand what it was all about at first.

When I first took Reiki One for myself, he would let me practice on him and sometimes he would come home from work and we would have dinner and we would sit down on the sofa together and my hands would automatically start to get warm (*the healing would automatically activate*) so rather than waste this beautiful energy I would place my hands on him intuitively. Eventually he would offer his elbow and ask me to put my hands there, or sit between my knees on the floor and lay my hands on the back of his neck. One of our daughters who lived at home would also have Reiki's and our other daughter also (*my step daughter*) who are both open to receiving.

My other daughters lived in England they too received healing when we visited England. And later on when I became a teacher, I attuned my eldest daughter Amanda and my youngest daughter Kate, which we will talk about later.

We think that to some extent that we have things planned out and in control in the physical world, but of course we don't! The contract we sign in the spiritual world, is for our souls/spirits growth and does not recognise pain, so we put our hands up for all sorts of things like a small child, because we know on the other side it will help our soul's growth.

We were making plans to return to England and by now realised that we will not be returning to live in the immediate future. This meant selling the property in England and telling my 2 eldest daughters not an easy thing to do.

# *Trip to England 2001*

*W*e booked the flights to England and I left in the November and we arranged for Mike to arrive Boxing Day, departing Christmas Day from Melbourne.

It was during this time that my mother began getting very confused and not recognising people this was of cours the onset of Dimentia. My brother Pete had moved her into a temporary rehabilitation centre as she wasn't coping in her own home. Previously she would ring my brother at all hours of the night worried about what was happening, he would need to dress and head down there to assure her everything was ok. Making all of the care decisions was taking its toll on my younger brother and therefore he gave the decision making of what nursing home she would be moved to up to myself and my older brother Mark.

Once I arrived Mark and I set about finding a nice place for her to stay in, as hard as it was we all knew it was for the best as she needed round the clock care. Occasionally she would ask when she was going home, and those times were the hardest. I stayed with my daughter Jane, her husband and the grandchildren which was special as it was the first time I was to meet my grandson. I really enjoyed baking and helping get things ready for Christmas which also took my mind off things.

Christmas Day arrived and is was very special. My eldest daughter travelled up from outside London with my two other grandchildren and I remember feeling so enriched having everyone together, all except Kate as she was in Australia at the time with friends. Oddly enough, earlier in the day I had a vision out of the blue of Amanda speeding to get to us that made me feel very uneasy. With that, the phone rang and it was her. I told her my thoughts and asked her to drive safely, luckily she reassured me that she had just seen a police car as a sign she should slow down. Angel signs!

The day was really lovely, until receiving a phone call later that night from Mike's Aunties partner saying she had been rushed to hospital. With Mike arriving the next day we had planned to stay with them and she had been preparing a turkey in the oven when the incident occurred. She had suffered a blood clot and complications from that which unfortunately resulted in her having part of her leg amputated. Once he arrived we headed straight round to their house, while Aunty was still in hospital we offered that we would like to stay and help to her partner which he was grateful for.

We travelled together to the hospital the next day to visit through the thick snow, it had been our first white Christmas in some time. When we arrived I was amazed at the good spirits she was in. She always has such a lovely, positive personality with the ability to find a joke in every situation, regardless of how dire it may seem from the outside. Her sense of humour is truly amazing, even in those circumstances!

I am pleased to say ten years later, Aunty is still around although getting quiet deaf and her eyesight is not so good now. Her partner is still a rock and looking after her very well indeed. Aunt's two daughters also keep an eye on things too, and grandchildren pay them visits, so all is good with them.

We spent New Year's Eve of that year at Jane's home with her in-laws and husband. That night my youngest grandson fell fast asleep across mine and Mike's lap, he was receiving Reiki and he looked so peaceful and content.

Whilst visiting my mother in the nursing home with my eldest daughter Amanda who is also a Reiki channel, we both stood either side of mother holding her hands and allowing the Reiki to flow through us into her. It was then she looked up at both of us took a knowing look and said "you can tell you two are sisters".

On my last visit to see my mother I went on my own and was helping her get into bed when she looked up at me and said 'I do believe you know'. It took a while for me to register what had just been said, as this was the women that chastise me for going to a spiritual church when my hip was really bad. It was shortly after this I asked the angels to not let her linger here. I had been a nurse years before and the thought of her getting bed sores was not what I wanted for her. I would ask God, if she is going to go, please make it quick, always giving thanks.

Mum passed away three months later.

# The Cash Dispenser

### Reiki Two Practitioner Level

### 2002

$\mathcal{I}$t was Mikao Usui's wish that this healing be available to each and every one of us.

After three months true to my word I took Reiki Two practitioner level, known as 'Inner Teachings'. My teacher would always wait at least three months after Reiki One. The reason being you personally undergo changes as your vibration rises and everything needs to settle down. Reiki One attunements are the main ones, and in alignment with Mikaro Usui's wish you are not allowed to ask for a fee with Reiki One, only when you take advanced Reiki are you allowed to charge a fee for giving Reiki to others. It's a dream of mine that everyone at some time would be attuned to Reiki One, people from all walks of life as the foundation of this healing is Unconditional Love and Universal Life Force and the regular Reiki practice to one another, of giving and the receiving of Reiki. That way we would keep our mind, body and soul well balanced, making better decisions and lifestyle changes. Reiki Two is about a journey of inner knowing or working with your intuition.

First day of Reiki Two a discussion takes place about Reiki One and a recap on what you did back then and why you wish to take it further. Beginning with a small meditation at the start of each workshop, it is always necessary to ground and centre yourself. You learn about three symbols, what their meanings are and how they feel as you practice each one individually, in other words getting to know them well. If you have not been attuned to Reiki One it doesn't matter how many times you use the symbols, it will not have any effect, and it's important to mention at this point that attunements cannot be taken off the internet they must be passed on from teacher to student. Learning more about the chakras on a deeper level you learn how to send distant healing on a more personal level and tap into their energy to release emotional issues, although this can only happen if the person gives you permission.

And it's a good idea to make a healing box with the Reiki Two symbols inscribed inside.

My youngest daughter would come home after school and if a friend was sick or a relative of a friend was ill, she would say can I put them in the healing box, the answer was always yes. When you work with energy it is so powerful and most times they will get better in some way or their health would improve.

People would come to our home for Reiki or Energy Balance Massage on a regular basis one of which was a beautiful Asian lady who worked in real estate, a neighbour, her daughter and also councillors would come for healings. A friend with whom I did a lot of workshops with thought it would be a good idea to start our own healing place by hiring a room somewhere. Just in a small way as we both had other responsibilities. We found a place within half an hour's drive from where we both lived. And together we worked from there on a Wednesday morning giving meditations and EBM (energy balance massages) and Reiki's whenever they were requested.

Our time there was one of spiritual growth not only for the both of us, but for the people who attended the meditation. We climbed some stairs at the back of the shop which gave us direct access to our room and in the front was a lady who was a practitioner in Hypnosis. The underneath was a fish and chip shop, and all of this was owned by the practitioner. The fish shop had changed hands many times and when the last owners decided to leave the lady who owned the building was deciding whether to open an alternative shop selling crystals, books and providing extra rooms for different practitioners who worked with alternative therapies. After much soul searching she made the decision to go ahead with the shop. In the meantime the lady whose shop it was, was concerned about the energies that had been left in the fish shop as it had changed hands quiet a lot of times. She asked if we would do a clearing on the premises and gave us the key to go there when it was empty. This we did the following week and as we stood there drawing the sacred Reiki Symbols, the two of us were totally amazed at the amount of energy that was leaving our hands this went on for quite a while, we asked the owner to allow the energies to settle for a few days before starting alterations on the shop.

We practised natural healing and teaching for a few years, and it was during this time of working together with people from our meditation group and patients that came in through the shop, that we gained some wonderful experiences, of which I would like to share with you who are reading this book.

As we were once setting up for our group meditation in the centre we worked, a mother came in with her son who was about 20yrs old. The lady was very distraught as her son was looking for some direction in life. He wore a lot of dark make up and dressed in gothic type clothes and was in an emotionally dark place. Seeing the look on her face as she walked away I ran after her and without a second thought told her not to worry we will bring him into the light. The words came out of my mouth before I had even thought about them! In the meditation I was guided to give him a clear quartz crystal (as we also worked with crystals). Over the weeks that followed, he attended regularly and changed very subtly. First his makeup came off, then his clothes became lighter and he started to wear a lot of white also. This beautiful young man then went on to take Reiki One and Reiki Two with us. His mother also started to attend meditation and healing with us. She eventually opened her own alternative therapies shop in Melbourne. Most of the people who came to the meditation group took Reiki One and Two with us! We have also given talks on the subject.

After taking Reiki Two, I had no interest in taking it further as I was quiet content with what I had learnt and now understood. It was to be a few years later that I decided to take the mastership and it was series of events that tested me on the lead up that brought me to this decision.

The first was when I was at the hairdresser and a mother with a small child came in. The little girl was about two or three years of age and a car had just accidently run over her foot only slightly fortunately she had some good strong shoes on. Naturally, the mother was very upset and the little girl was crying. My reaction was doing what I found naturally and even though my hair was wet, I got out of the chair I was sitting in and went over to the little girl to offer my help. The hairdresser had already explained to the mother that I am a Reiki practitioner and so it was alright to go ahead. I place my hands on the little girl's foot, at first she kept taking my hands off, eventually letting me place them there for a while and when I went to take my hands off, she got hold of them and placed my hands back on her foot.

The next experience was to be some months later, my husband and I were out shopping and a lady who was large in stature stumbled down a step and was unable to get up again as she was in so much pain with her knee. When I saw her, even though there were people passing by, I walked over to her and placed my hands on her knee for about five minutes, until I felt it was OK for her to get up. When she got to her feet I asked her to take a couple of anti-inflammatory tablets when she got home to assist. These were tests for me and it was then that I suddenly realised that I should continue my journey of Reiki and take my Mastership giving me the qualifications to teach Reiki. Taking the previous courses in Energy Balance Massage and a Diploma in Holistic Counselling gave me the tools and empathy to help and heal others.

In my lifetime I have had many jobs ranging from working in retail, nursing, personal assistant in a financial institution a bakers, telephone sales for a sports company to working as a doctor's receptionist, yet through all of this none really seemed to 'fit'. It wasn't until I embarked on my spiritual journey at 50 years old that the pieces began to come together and I truly felt I had indeed found my calling.

# *Facing My Fears*

*To* add another job to the list, I decided to undertake volunteer care work during this time and through the agency I reached out to became a carer for a young lady who had just turned forty and had been diagnosed with Schizophrenia.

*(When I was about eight years old, I remember watching my Aunt on my fathers side, who the family also believed had Schizophrenia yet had passed over many years ago. My Aunt would talk and laugh out loud to herself even when people were in the room it made no differnce she was in a world of her own. One time when staying the night at my Nanna's they asked me to sleep in the same bed as my my Aunt, which I assume as company for her for a couple of nights. I was really frightened, because of what I had seen for myself as a small child. But she did say to me on one of the nights I was staying there, was that "I haven't always been like this". We were holidaying in a caravan and some heavy pans dropped on her head. It was also true that she wanted children yet unfortunately they found out that her husband couldn't have any children. Eventually he agreed to adoption and then changed his mind at the very last minute. This they say, tipped the balance and my Aunty was diagnosed as Schizophrenic.*

*My cousin who is a well know clairvoyant, and has always had the gift, told me my Aunt was a beautiful lady and a clairvoyant herself and showed my cousin when she was a young girl, how she could switch lights on and off with her mind. And that people would come and ask her for readings regularly. The sad part in all of this, is that it was a very long time ago and people would come to her and ask her things and then through their own fear begin to ridicule and reject her, this in turn led to her having a nervous breakdown and also contributed to the diagnosis of Schizophrenia.*

Back to my young lady of forty with whom I used to take out once a week. This lady suffered brain damage at birth through lack of oxygen and although she was generally really good, she was just a little slow. Unfortunately in her younger years she was allowed to live with a man who became physically abusive towards her in a horrific ways, which led to the diagnosis of Shizophrenia.

On my first time out with Carol I went to pick her up in the car and her mother told me that her balance wasn't very good due to the medication she was receiving. Her mother would often talk to me that she longed for the 'old' Carol back. On my second visit I asked her mother's permission to give her Reiki at home, which she agreed and I did this in front of her mother. The week that followed I received a phone call from Carol's mother to say she was taking her to the doctors as there was a clot just inside her eye. Knowing that she had had a Reiki, I asked her to try and not worry too much as it was making its way out at the nearest exit point'. The doctor reassured them both everything was fine. From that day forward Carol would ask for Reiki's on a regular basis and eventually her medication was reduced and her mother began to get the old Carol back.

## Mothers Children and Pets

I was surrounded at this time with young mothers and children all of whom were friends. It was nothing for them to come to me on a regular basis for Reiki's and occasionally I would also counsel them holistically. I always felt that giving Reiki to a person is a privilege, and I was honoured that they allowed me to do these healings. One mother stopped coming to visit as she was busy, and then fell pregnant with her third baby. When she was about 22 weeks, the doctors discovered the unborn baby had a growth in the lower area of his body. When the mother went back a week later it had doubled its size. This lead to one of the young mothers in the group encouraging her to come and see me, explaining she had nothing to lose. She then began to come on a regular basis.

The first session went really well for both mother and baby. They both seemed to be receiving the healing very well indeed a visit to the hospital under examination the growth had stopped growing. This beautiful pregnant mother received treatment once a week until the baby was born. After the baby was born one or two small lumps appeared on the baby's head and the mother asked the nurses if it was acceptable for me to come and give Reiki. Permission was given allowing me to give Reiki's in the nursery and while thankfully they later disappeared. The only thing was that there was not much movement from his hip area. I would accompany the mother and baby regularly on visits to the hospital. And the amazing thing is when you are working with a higher intelligence through Reiki, your hands would automatically connect to that person who needs the healing, and this time it was baby who was sitting in the back seat on the way to the hospital. The drive took us about forty five minutes so he would get his fill of healing and I would always say when my hands were activated to the Angels/Higher Intelligence. '**Let this healing go to whoever needs it and may it be received for their highest will and good**' remembering to always say thank you, for it will be so.

One particular time we were visiting the hospital, the baby's mother was very tired, so I took him in his pushchair for a walk around the hospital to let his mother gets some rest. It was during this walk that he was sat facing forward and he couldn't see me, so I thought perfect time for me to use some Reiki symbols over his head without him knowing. As soon as I started to draw the symbols, Daniel without even looking up reached up with his hand and pushed my hand away from him with such force. It was then I realised I had gone as far as I was allowed to go as far as his healing was concerned and that this was part of his Sacred Contract. The lessons that he has agreed to learn for his soul's growth, although probably at that time of talking it over with his counsellors on the other side, you don't think too much about the physical body and how it will feel on a daily basis. I must finish by saying that the outcome was good, because during that time of travelling with mother/baby to the hospital, they went from saying tumour, to saying a lump until they couldn't find anything. He will be about twelve now and to this day he plays wheel chair basketball, and because he hasn't been operated on, his mother is still looking forward to the day when he can be given the opportunity of successful stem cell treatment.

My Reiki partner and I continued to treat people on a regular basis sometimes at the place we gave meditations and sometimes at our homes. Some of which would be counsellors themselves, you see in listening to others you can without realising absorb the problems, which are as we term lower thoughts and leave a person who is listening feeling really drained. We do advise them to protect themselves, by putting themselves in a bubble of white light or a tube of pink light, remembering that all thought is energy and that's what you create for yourself in a loving way.

Going back to the place where we gave meditations we continued for a few years, until my partner decided she didn't want to do it any more as her personal life became very busy. Although I could have kept it going on my own I made a conscious decision not to as for me, it didn't feel right. And after all you have do what is in your heart and mind what sits right with you. To this day the shop is still a natural therapies shop.

# *Reiki Mastership 2004*

As mentioned earlier it was a series of events that led to my taking the Reiki mastership course.

The little girl at the hairdressers and the lady falling off a step, were both realisations that I was ready to continue my personal journey.

For me it was all about living my truth and honouring who I was by doing what I hold dear in my heart, which is healing. Then passing that knowledge onto others. Reiki itself is a journey of the soul. The point that I settled on my realisation to continue my Reiki journey was a beautiful sunny day and I was sitting outside in the sunshine when my phone rang. It was my Reiki Master/Teacher and she was calling to talk with me about taking my learnings further in the exact moment I was confident in my decision to do so, this was only further confirmation.

So my journey continued, I saw my teacher a once a week for about six to eight months which during this time you learn and experience a great deal. Learning more about the symbols as angels communicate through symbols and thoughts and the journey is remarkable. Each week you practice a symbol, sometimes two on your pillow at home each night.

During this time I was asked to speak at an event at the care centre where I worked as a volunteer about meditation and natural healing. A week leading up to my speaking event I was practising a certain symbol before bed when I had the most vivid dream. It was of a beautiful woman on horseback and the horse and the woman seemed as though they were one. The colours that they adorned were yellow and brown wide wavy stripes, and it was in Canada with tall pine trees and in the background was clear blue skies.

Later that week I gave my talk on meditation and healing to a lot more people than I had expected. All went well which was a relief and as they were leaving a beautifully dressed lady with curley long golden blonde hair caught my eye as she was dressed in the same colours that I had seen in my vision in the dream. She stood up to leave and as she did looked me straight in the eye from the back of the room, as people began to leave around her she gave me a slow nod of the head and a knowing smile. Just then another lady came up to talk to me and I had to look away and when I looked up again she had gone.

You don't always experience something as I did with the lady on the horse with each symbol but it is important to always stay open to receiving what is appropriate for you.

I remember going to one of my Mastership sessions at my teacher's home when she stood up, went over to her table and picked up a statue of Quin Yin placing it in my hands. I was surprised as I knew that I hadn't ordered one it felt symbolic, as I had never thought of the female aspect of God and it really made me look at things from both a male/female perspective. After all just as we have male/female in us and as we are made in our Creators image, surely he has too!

As time went on in my mastership I took the magnified healing course and was initiated to learn about the Goddess Quan Yin. She is the mother of mercy, compassion and forgiveness and works with the violet flame. Believe me, I struggled with the female Goddess for a couple of years, having always believed that God could only be male and masculine. From early beginnings and understanding of the bible there was never discussion of a female goddess which I suppose is where those ingrained beliefs to overcome came from. Even though during the meditation for the initiation process whilst my teacher was reading the transmission Quan Yin come from what appeared to be behind my teacher around the back of us and gave us the initiation personally. To quote Sylvia Browne in her first book she wrote 'God is the static one who holds everything in its place the logical one just like most males, then the female part of God is the emotional side'. And as human beings each one of us experiences some emotion one way or another we are experiencing for our creator and that has to be good. Remember nothing lasts forever and we always come through crises in our lives if we just learn patience and talk to your creator, because you will always be heard. You might not get your answers straight away, or the one you were expecting, but you will get them when the time is right for you to know.

During my Mastership course I attended many Reiki workshops and also a children's' Reiki attunements, which was a day course and was kept very playful with drawings and bubble blowing.

The initiation to Reiki/Mastership and introduction to magnified healing felt like a very sacred experience, amplified from the direct experience with Quan Yin.

# 2005 Trip To England

$\mathcal{N}$ ovember 27th 2005

I travelled back to England on my own this time. I can't remember ever feeling more anticipation and excitement at seeing the family that the journey felt like it took forever. It was due to my eagerness to get there that everything seemed to be going wrong and delaying the journey. Leaving Melbourne the plane was delayed about forty minutes and being I had already arrived three hours early at Melbourne airport, only made things worse. Then a late arrival at Heathrow meant we missed our landing slot, resulting in another ten minute delay and then had to be towed in meaning another fifteen minute delay. Getting off the plane my legs were walking so fast, I was nearly running. When I reached the baggage control, it was then that because I was one of the first passengers on the plane, my luggage was the last off.I was excited, overwhelmed and frustrated all at the same time. I was desperate to see my family. Rushing through the green 'nothing to declare' sign and finally seeing my eldest daughter Amanda together with the two eldest grandchildren, nothing else mattered. Holding my daughter so tight tears of joy flowed. I had been so worried about her and the grandchildren as Amanda was going through a divorce and of course these things are never easy. It was my aim that while I was there I could at least help them feel that everything will be alright in the end.

My grandchildren each had a Reiki whilst I was there and it was done in a very gentle discreet way. My eldest grandson David came for a cuddle on the settee with his Nan that evening, and I intuitively placed one of my hands on his tummy. I could feel the energy flowing and he sat there so relaxed. When David went to bed, during the night, he had woken up because he was having this vivid dream. (*Emotional blockage being released*). He saw his stomach area (*sacral chakra*) expanding and all 'black stuff being pushed out' - his words. My eldest granddaughter too experienced some emotional release after her Reiki. I was privileged to take Amanda through her Reiki One attunements, just before Christmas whilst I was over there. It was truly a wonderful experience for both of us. After preparing the room, I started by taking her through a guided meditation to bring in the light and tears rolled down her cheeks. I opened my eyes briefly to see this, and her eyes were closed, as a mother I wanted to get up and cuddle her, but knew I had to carry on with the meditation. After the meditation I asked how she felt. Amanda said she saw a bright white light entering her and an overwhelming sense of peace, and her face one of amazement as she connected to the Divine which was beautiful to witness. The energies that day were very powerful as they swirled around us and it held such sacred moments. The children were particularly good as they sat quietly in the other room watching television, we explained to them what we would be doing and we took the workshop over two days, a week apart. A few months after I returned to Australia I received an excited text from Amanda, saying that she had just had an amazing experience. She explained that she had gone up into David's room to check on him and thought to send her son healing whilst sleeping. So she stood some distance away as not to disturb him and turned the palms of her hands towards him, when she saw this beautiful blue light coming from her hands, it wasn't long after that, that her son just sat bolt upright in bed, he was obviously feeling the energy. God the Father/Mother God, Our Creator, Angelic Realm, Higher Intelligence, Universal Life Force, all Light Beings Mikao Usual Quan Yin, or whoever you prefer to name and connect with, are just fantastic once you have tapped in to their energy. They are all aspects of God/Goddess and to be greatly honoured and respected.

# Amanda's Marriage Break-down

*A*manda, her husband and the children moved to town in Leicestershire, a beautiful country town steeped in history.

While Kate and I had moved to Australia, I would try to get back on an average every eighteen months to see the family. I travelled on my own quiet a lot at first, my husband was busy working and Kate was settled in her new school. I needed to get my fill with my family as it wasn't easy for me to settle, I had lived in England for fifty years. It was on one of these visits that I could see Amanda wasn't happy, but I couldn't just come out with it. One day after we had eaten and the children were in bed, we sat at the table across from one another on our own in the dining room whilst her husband separated from us in another room watching television as he often would. Amanda faced me and, I reached out to hold her hands, we looked each other in the eyes, and she began to cry and cry. Not word was spoken between us, as it didn't have to be. I knew.

Before I left I wrote a letter to make her feel strong and asked her to keep being strong whatever decision she made.

Their marriage came to an end after about seventeen years ironically about the same time as my own. Amanda is a kind, loving human being who considers everyone else's needs first. Her husband spent most of their marriage working nights as this suited him, but ultimately left Amanda to raise the children up on her own. She never really had the support of her husband, they didn't interact as a family and any trips

Amanda made back to her hometown with the children was usually without her husband which was over a four hour drive. Eventually she became all used up and the glass was empty. Once the decision had been made, her husband did admit that he hadn't worked hard enough for their relationship to work and took full responsibility for where things had landed which was appreciated at the time.

Amanda eventually found her own house for her and the two children. While they were now separated Amanda was supported by her ex-husband should the children start to get out of hand as they were likely to do during a time of such upheaval.

They have now both grown and are now a credit to their mother and father. They were able to sort things out with their children and come to sensible conclusions, not to say the children as with most divorced couples were affected in some way or other. In the beginning David felt some responsibility to suddenly become the man of the house although he was only fourteen years old at that time. His sister Kylie craved the attention of a father who was never home to spend good quality time with her. She has since become a mother to Oscar her son, who is a very loving soul and I know he is someone who will be really loved and taken care of. David is also very protective towards them, and they are very supportive of one another.

# New South Wales Australia

In 2006, Mike and I were visiting friends in a country town in N.S.W and stayed in there guest house at the back of their property. We would go for drives and often look at land and house builds as ultimately we knew we wanted to move away from the city of Melbourne for a more relaxed life. By this point in time I had come to the realisation that we wouldn't be returning to England in the short term as was originally planned, it had already been five years. This made things very hard with my family back home as of course my daughters were not happy with the change in plan, although it was never my intention to leave for any longer than the 2years I had first said. Circumstances held us in Australia and we worked to get ahead financially as much as possible. One of my daughters denied my existence for a while, ignoring calls and birthday cards until eventually calling to tell me how she was feeling. Ultimately she was heartbroken that I wouldn't be returning home, yet wanted me to also be happy. We spoke at length and talked through all of her concerns and worked things through and eventually understood.

So after five years, we sold the house in England which, along with Mike's hard work financed our way to purchasing property and land along the Murray River. Mike worked almost seven days a week since our arrival in Australia, dedicated to our lives together and without this we never would have achieved what we managed. We both wanted the same things out of life and love one another very much that we could weather all the storms which has ultimately lead us to the lovely place we have now found ourselves in.

I digress…Back to where we were staying at the guest house, at the rear of our friends property. On one of our drives I told Mike that I realised I knew where he wanted to live, however he had never asked me the same thing, I think he was surprised as it had never been raised before but he was keen to hear. I told him that I knew it was a long shot, but somewhere up high ideally overlooking the ocean.

That being said we continued to look for property in the area. Soon after we were driving through nearby town, to where we were staying when a sign advertising land for sale appeared on the side of the road. We drove past but reversed to look again with the intention of checking it out.

We drove down a windy road, following it to the top of a hill where four blocks of land were for sale, however one of them had a 'reserved' sign on. Not perturbed at this point and purely out of interest we called the real estate agent to enquire.,

The agent said as the reserved sign was only on one and they had just gone up for sale being prime real estate it was likely the others would sell fast he explained the situation and if it was something we wanted to do, then we needed to leave a deposit right then and there with the remainder payable in three months.

We made the decision on the spot and took the chance hoping that the powers that be, were looking after us – and it turns out they were! Within the next three weeks we managed to sell both the block of land and the house along the Murray and had enough for our deposit. All just fell into place.

It was to be another three years before we built as my husband was unsure about leaving his job in Melbourne, as his job afforded us a good lifestyle. I couldn't push the situation, even though I was ready to go then and there! It was a case of waiting until he felt ready as it was a big decision for him to make and therefore it had to be when it felt right for him. In the meantime I kept up with giving Reiki's and Energy Balance Massages.

# 2007 Back To the U.K.

England August/September and Reiki Two

*I* again travelled back to the UK on my own as my husband was busy working and really didn't want to leave our dear dog.

It was my eldest granddaughter's christening, she was thirteen years old. Amanda had moved into her own home and it still needed a bit of freshening up with some paint, so we both set about doing the painting that needed to be done, including the lounge and dining room. The grandchildren were really good, as I set about doing the decorating whilst Amanda was at work, she would then start when she arrived home, and the grandchildren cooked us the meals. It was very sweet.

The day of the Christening arrived, it was a Sunday and a beautiful sunny day. Before leaving we prepared the food and placed it on the table ready for when guests arrived back after my grandaughter had been christened eveything went off as planned.

Amanda's ex-sister-in-law was staying with us as she was visiting from out of town for the Christening. She was a lovely lady and sadly had been seeing psychologists for a number years about her depression. She confided that she could never remember anything of her childhood from when she was a little girl. It so happened that a time and space was made available to us to talk properly and for all the goings on it was amazing as we were not disturbed once, again I believe this was the higher sources intervention. I took her through a small meditation and it was then that I knew she would benefit greatly from having a Reiki, coupled with that I was beginning to take my daughter through Reiki Two and this could be excellent practise for her. Amanda asked me to work with her and it was my intuition that three sessions would be required.

The first session there was a lot of coughing this happened when on her heart chakra, which relates to mother father, husband or partner, it can happen on different chakras. After the session she said she was feeling great for the rest of the day. It was in the second session the following day, that my holistic counselling skills came into play. Whilst Amanda was at her feet and I was working on the head, I took her back to the day she was born onwards and slowly brought her forward which led to her talking about her childhood that she had been suppressing for many years. Lot of crying proceeded as she released all of those emotions of past experiences. This was a major breakthrough for her, and it turned out that when she was very small her father would tell her time and time again that she should never have been born and shouldn't be here.'

We gave the final Reiki the next day and once we were finished gave her some mindful exercises to complete and a mediation CD. As far as we both know, so far so good.

# *2009*

*T*wo years later in July of 2009 my eldest daughter Amanda and her children were planning a trip to Australia. I was filled with joy at the thought of them all visiting us as they would be the second people to visit from my family my younger brother Pete and his wife being the first. It was Amanda's dream to see Uluru since she was about four years old, although this was the first time she had told me! My husband Mike offered to look after the children for a few days *(they were fifteen and seventeen years old)* whilst Amanda and I spent that time together at Uluru which was truly magical.

The first night was a dining out under the stars experience where we were greeted with a glass of champagne and sat watching the sun go down over the rock. There was no moon that night and it was pitch black, we had eaten our dinner and Amanda had new digital camera began taking photos of the darkness to see what might appear as orbs had appeared on her camera before and it wasn't until we got back to the hotel when seeing photo more closely I noticed the orb was an unusual colour and also quite dense. We decided to take them to get developed and to see how much they could enlarged the photo we received five enlargements in total at different stages and while you expect them to become more blurred with the increase of size they only become more clear. The clearer they became the more we were intrigued there were the colours and shapes it felt as though we had been priveldged and felt like a highly spiritual experience for both of us. It wasn't until sometime later that I opened one of my books by Sylvia Browne that I read about physics on the other side. It explained that a dimension on the other side can fit into a corner in one of our rooms it was at this point it all made sense to me.

While still in Australia my eldest grandson David had decided he wanted to get a tattoo. He had printed off some drawings from the computer and brought them through for our opinion. Being his Nan I wasn't overly keen on the idea and to demonstrate how it would look when he got older I screwed up the paper and gave it back to him. We both laughed as it was in jest, but didn't put him off. He has since had another but I guess for him this was a special thing to have done whilst in Australia. They stayed for only three weeks and, of course I wished it would have been a lot longer preferably to move over here, but it wasn't meant to be. They went back to England in early August and the next week that followed was when I got the go ahead from Mike to finally sell the house so we could move forward into our new life.

As Mike had taken so long to make this decision I wasted no time in contacting the real estate agent who had given us her details some years earlier. Mike had rang me up on his way home from work no doubt he had a challenging day, and the house was on the market before he arrived in the driveway – no time to waste! The realtors were through the next day and within three weeks we had three offers on the table, things were happening in three's! An offer was accepted with a 30 day settlement and we were on our way. Kate had decided to travel indefinitely overseas at this time so after saying goodbye to her at the airport, we headed up to begin our next chapter.

For the next three months life was hectic once again we stayed in our friend's guest house where we had previously stayed whilst our house was being built, until we were eventually given our move in date of December the 16th. I couldn't wait. While it had been very generous of them to allow us to stay on their property they were unfortunately going through a marriage breakdown and separation which landed us right in the middle of the turmoil. Times were tense to say the least and we aimed to be up and out early most days as unfortunately our friends wife wasn't speaking to us, believing we were taking her husband side.

Ultimately we were just trying to remain neutral and listen to both sides of the breakup which inevitably there were to be no winners, in hindsight we should have just remained very separate from it all.

The move in day finally arrived and it couldn't have ran smoother. Thankfully our friend helped us with moving and settling our things which we were very grateful for. The carpets were down, the blinds hung on every window and believe it or not we had unpacked everything on the very same day - finished and put away.

When we had finished, we stood on the veranda, looked back into the lounge room and felt in complete awe of how everything had perfectly come together. All the furniture we had purchased remotely fit and looked fantastic. We had created all this with our Angels as we could not have done it on our own. They know you better than you think you know yourself and dream come true.

A good way to ask your Angels guidance when making decisions is to say *"You know me better than I know myself, please sort it out for me"* in other words just turn your decisions over to them and your answer will appear.

# Beginning Life In New South Wales Australia 2010

$\mathcal{S}$itting in the shade on our new veranda overlooking the ocean on a beautiful sunny day, I was already thinking of where I might place some information on Reiki and meditation in the local town that people may see and pick up. Before making the move I had imagined how my life might look in our new home town and visualised meditation groups and one on one Reiki healing sessions and slowly but surely things started to come together. As we work with a higher intelligence we just need to make our intention clear, create the space and allow the opportunities to come with a little patience and trust that things will come together.

My first client was a young mother with three boys who had just moved up to where we lived to escape an abusive drug related relationship, knowing no one in the area at the time. She saw my notice of information about Reiki outside the newspaper shop and gave my number a call to arrange a time to visit. I remember how she looked when I opened the door, very thin and her face very troubled. The remarkable thing is that after a Reiki session she physically looked as though a huge weight had been lifted from her. I wouldn't allow her to pay me as I felt privileged to have had the opportunity to have helped her. This young mother would come for Reiki's whenever she felt the need and would occasionally bring a thank you gift whenever she could afford to. Sometimes you have to listen to what you know in your heart to be right. This young mother came whenever she needed help and support, even joining the meditation group, which eventually led her to take Reiki One. This has helped her through many a troubled time. Her two eldest sons have found their own way in life due to the right guidance given from their mother, the other boy is much younger and is doing well at school.

# *2011 Trip To England*

$\mathcal{A}$ year later around Easter time I decided it was time to take my beloved husband away for a long deserved break and we headed up to Sydney as neither of us had been before.

Earlier that year my youngest grandson Henry who was 9yrs old had started having problems with pain in his left hip on seeing the doctor was told it may take a couple of years, but could recover on its own His parents, were not satisfied and took him for a second opinion and it was then that my youngest grandson was diagnosed as having Perthes disease. His parents were given a choice of having a fixator attached to his leg to adjust his hip into place, or let it repair naturally and they decided on the fixator. This was put into place and some pins were drilled into his leg. The whole process was to take four months from beginning, to rehabilitation and eventually expected full recovery but would require a lot of work in between. My daughter Jane and her husband contacted us whilst we were away on that Easter weekend to see if we would return to England and look after Henry and of course, we immediately said yes (although it meant I would be going alone as Mike needed to work) and that I would stay for as long as they needed me. Dates and times were arranged and put into place within the next week.

Four years had passed since I had last visited my family in England, because we had moved interstate and financially couldn't afford it at the time. However, I kept in touch with phone calls and the occasional Skype, although I didn't see the children on Skype whenever I spoke to my daughter being in England the timing was all wrong as they were still young and therefor would be in bed, I really missed them.

I arrived in England on June 1st 2011 and my youngest grandson had had his operation a few days before. My eldest daughter picked me up from Heathrow airport with my eldest granddaughter with whom I stayed for a couple of days while I recovered from my jet lag. As Amanda was working we couldn't get to Sheffield hospital until Friday night after she had finished work but she came straight from work picked us up and made the one hour thirty minutes drive to the hospital and returned home the same night. On arrival I was so anxious to see them my daughter and her husband were stood at Henry's bedside, I just gave my daughter the longest biggest hug I could muster not forgetting her husband and both the grandchildren.

Meanwhile my youngest daughter Kate, who also lives in Australia, thought it would be a good idea to surprise her sister Jane, her husband and the two children. It would be the first time that Kate would be seeing her nephew Henry and was really looking forward to it. Plans were put into place and we all had to keep mum for the next few months, which as most people know it is very difficult as you often have to check yourself before giving things away in conversation. In the meantime I went back with my son-in-law and youngest grandaughter to prepare for Henry's home coming.

The next day my daughter her husband and grandson came home.

Henry just quietly got on with things watching lots of D.V.D's in the beginning although I would give him Reiki's at every opportunity to help speed up the healing process he was very brave. As night after night he had to suffer so much pain having his dressings changed. His parents really were wonderful with him, and I am very proud of them.

When Kate arrived she brought her best friend Tilly with her, who is like family to us in Australia, and naturally she wanted to meet Kate's family in England.

On the day of their arrival, Kate let me know where they were, and I made myself scarce, going out giving them space for their arrival. I parked the car where I could see the house but they couldn't see me and waited for them to arrive. They knocked on the door and Jane opened it, the look of surprise was something I will always remember, lots of big hugs took place I felt warm inside watching them.

As Kate had arrived and hadn't been back home in some time it was decided that a family party at their house would be a great way of seeing everyone. We set about organising everything buying the food and cleaning the house in readiness for the party.

It wasn't long after this that Kate, Tilly and myself went to stay with my eldest daughter Amanda for a week she lived around two hours away so we packed up the car and headed off (although Kate and her friend only had 3 weeks it went all too quickly).

When the time came to return to Australia we all said our goodbyes hugged everyone and thanked them for our time spent together all that is except my youngest grandaughter who didn't won't to know me this time around it broke my heart spending over 3 months of rejection from her.

# Returning To Australia

*W*e returned to Australia that same week, Kate and Tilly on the Tuesday and myself on the Thursday. My grief continued for some time over what happened and it wasn't until eighteen months later when arranging a return trip to England that I began to heal.

While this time I was returning with my husband as I no longer wanted to go alone and felt I needed his loving support, the thought of again being so close to the drama and the heartache filled me with dread. As we booked our flights around six months out from when we were due to leave. I continued meditating on it and writing unsent letters, placing them in my healing box. It was on one of these meditations, that I had a turning point. It was though I had travelled down to the bottom and things suddenly took an upturn swing. I knew at that moment, whatever was said by Vikki or her mother, wouldn't hurt me anymore. It really was a strange feeling, but a satisfying one. Of course, I still love them unconditionally and would welcome them back into my arms at any given time, but I had managed to find peace with what was out of my control. I relate this emotion to the unconditional love we all have inside of us. As we are part of our Creator a part of the whole/oneness there nothing that is ever said or done in your life as you learn and grow, will stop there unconditional love for you.

It is important to recognise that we as humans have both male and female characteristics and so too has our Creator. Sometimes we need to make our feminine side to be more dominant or visa versa depending on our circumstances.

We are here to learn different lesson and once we learn a lesson by saying to ourselves 'I will make sure that lesson won't happen again,' it is only then we can then move on to the next one and its how we handle the situations we are presented with that in turn helps your Creator to experience.

It is important to remember that in the tough times we keep moving forward as nothing lasts forever and the tough times will pass. Everything that happens to us is only temporary and in the scheme of things this lifetime is very short.

# *Phenomenum*

*L*iving in Australia gave me the freedom to pursue the things that I enjoy the most and it was my husband that encouraged me to spread my wings. I practised meditation regularly and also started a small group at home. It was during one of these meditations and over many months that I noticed one of ladies physical appearance seemed to be dwindling and it seemed her energy was slowly depleting, she was beginning to take on a 'haunted' look and I was starting to get concerned. It was around this time that this particular lady had suggested holding the meditation circle in the yurt she had in the back garden of her home. (This is a circular building made up of approximately 9 to 12 sides that went to an apex at the top) Everyone agreed as it seemed like a good spot and when the day arrived, without thinking, I grabbed a clear quartz to take with me. I held the quartz in my hand as I guided the others through the meditation. During the session (which involves bringing in the white light and clearing the chakras) I let the angels guide us on a beautiful journey. The standard sequence for the meditation usually involves bringing in the white light then clearing the chakras from the crown down. This time however when we reached the bottom two I could see with my mind's eye that this energy was being taken from me, it swirled around the sacral chakra and the base and then pierced the earth with great force, and while I did manage to take control it was quite demanding. After the meditation we would generally turn some angel cards and then talk about whatever came up,. Yet this particular time was different and two of the younger ladies became irate at each other. The energies were quite negative and really became uncomfortable this was unusual as the conversations are usually very loving and caring.

We left the ladies yurt and later that week each person spoke to me individually and said how they had felt uncomfortable during the session in the yurt. I instinctively knew that it was the yurt that was effecting this particular ladys energy, although I didn't want to frighten her so in line with divine timing waited until the time felt right.

After pondering the best way to approach this without causing her concern I eventually decided to call her and asked her to consult with her pendulum on 3 seperate occassions as to whether the yurt was draining her energy. She responded well and as a spiritual person agreed, if only to appease me I would think.

Unsurprisingly around four days later, she called me back telling me that the pendulum acknowledged my concerns and confirmed this was in fact the case. Further to this she asked whether I would clear it, understanding I would be able to through asking the pendulum. The first thought that came to mind was I felt privileged that God and the Angels had asked me to take part in the cleansing, and I never doubted that it had to be done. Intuitively I knew that it required three seperate clearings and organised for the first session to commence three days later on the Monday.

Coincidently (or not as nothing is coincidence!) my cousin Sally, who is an international clairvoyant from the UK called to chat on the Sunday night before. While we didn't always talk about spirituality, this time I asked if she would be open to it as the next days events were weighing heavily on my mind. During the conversation and my filling her in on what was going on, she assured me that Archangel Metatron was working with me and not to fear. She made the situation clearer to me of what was going on as I was working purely from trust.

It was important to be reminded of that point that as a light worker we are not alone and always supported by the Angelic Realm.

Monday arrived and before I left I talked to God and the Angels, asking for the protection of white light and of the Holy Spirit that morning and also Quan Yins Magnified Healing process before I left the house. I left with my radio, cd's and a candle as I knew this lady had already used white sage in the morning before I arrived. As I knew the lady had previously been attuned to Reiki Two, I asked her to assist me outside the yurt and to draw some symbols at the same time as myself, before entering the yurt alone. Once inside I lit the candle, switched on the calming angelic music and as a Reiki Master/Teacher proceeded with all the symbols that intuitively came to mind. It was then that I met with some resistance as the radio would switch off all by itself, this happened a lot during the first session.

Afterwards my clairvoyant cousin told me that at the time I was working in the yurt, she was looking for me with her third eye but had trouble finding me at first, then saw me surrounded by energy. She then explained what she understood to have happened.

Someone had opened a vortex in the yurt, an opening that leads to another dimension which in turn was draining my friend of energy. My cousin told me it was this vortex that needed to be sealed and that it was my task to do so. This made me feel more comfortable with what was happening and gave me further insight into what was going on.

I returned on the Wednesday and used the same procedure and this time the radio went smoothly without being stopped and there was no interference which was when I knew the lower thought forms or energies had tried to stop this happening on the first day were fading away, or had potentially completely gone. Thankfully my friend in her words said that even after the first session she started to feel a lot lighter, which confirmed we were on the right path. Friday came for the final clearance and once I was finished I asked my dear friend not to go in it for a few days and to not allow anyone else to go in until the energies had settled.

After this period had passed a few days later, my friend went into her yurt and said she noticed a big difference and I also noticed that she looked a lot lighter. Within that same week she was back to her old bubbly, bright self and wanted me to cleanse her house.

The amount of people who came to my meditation group, would vary from two to six people for meditation, as it is casual, people would come whenever they felt the need. A place where you can talk about your concerns, both a sacred and a safe place. It is a healing place filled with love.

# Visit To England 2013

$I$t was March 2013, and we lost our beloved dog Jack. Jack was a small white dog and a cross between a Bichon Fresse and we were told a Maltese, although as he grew he looked as though he had some poodle in him. He was a real delight to us and brought us much happiness. It wasn't until Jack was nine years old that we learnt he had a heart problem, two years before he passed away. He'd developed a cough and we were told that it was one of the signs. When we thought back we remembered when we used to throw the ball for him as a puppy and after chasing it for about three times he would be exhausted and have to stop, then gradually over time the cough got worse. We had planned to go over to England in the coming May for six weeks, but were concerned as our dear dog was sick and his condition was worsening, which made us afraid to leave him. Although it may sound awful, I remember looking at him, believing our pets understand everything we say and explained how worried I was that something was to happen while we were away as I know we wouldn't have been able to forgive ourselves. I knew it would happen soon enough, I just hoped that it will be before we go.

He looked so ill and was getting slowly worse until one day we had to take him to the vet. By this stage he could hardly walk and was losing a lot of bodily fluid. The vet told us that his organs were breaking down and the kindest thing was to let him go to end his suffering. He gave us a day to talk to him and say our goodbyes and that night we took him on the beach as he loved the beach, and all he could do was just sit, he then walked up to Mike and sat beside him which was so sad to watch. I felt it was like he was saying "I can't do this anymore".

The next day we went to the vet and they were very compassionate, they said we will just place a port in him and you can go and sit in the back of your car with him and we will come out to you. Jack was laid across my knees and when the vet came she had no sooner put the fluid into the port that he went, it was so quick that he was truly ready, it didn't stop the tears from flowing. We took him and laid him down on his favourite rug, lit a candle and said our goodbyes and said to him 'see you later'. We have so much respect and love for our dear dog Jack and the unconditional love he brought was beyond words. We were so grateful to him for having the opportunity of sharing his life with us and we know that we will see him again.

We decided to extend our holiday to three months, and visit Italy whilst we were in Europe.

We spent time at Amanda's and always enjoyed staying there, seeing the eldest grandchildren, Amanda lived in a pretty village with lots of history. We then stayed at Mike sisters place with her and her daughter for a week, which was a delight then my brother Pete and his wife for a couple of days. And he suggested that we stay at my eldest brothers Mark house.

It was so good spending time with them, as we really hadn't spent a lot of time with my eldest brother in many years. And it was a special time and one I will cherish for they are people that come from love and at the end of the day, love is the most important thing. And we respected what they did and they in return respected us also, without judgement and that's so important. So we returned to Australia without seeing the youngest grandchildren for reasons explained in previous chapters that were still unresolved on their end.

# Karma and Patience Learned

## Sacred Contract

## 2015

Taking no notice of the warning signs sent from the Angels, remembering they don't know what pain is and will always do their upmost to protect us. We sit there on the other side with our counsellors and put plans into place for our Sacred Contract, we also don't know what pain is, we are spirit/energy and whole. Also we put our hands up for anything and everything and our counsellors say 'are you sure that you want to do that' and what do we do like children we say Yes! Because we know it will be for our souls growth, then off we go, down to this dark planet, to bring light upon it through our experiences.

This time I wasn't listening to the warning signs to slow down, I was caught up in the world and its fast paced way of life, not even bothering to meditate or balance my body through exercise not giving myself time to meditate even. And the events that followed were because I didn't sit with what I was doing and not taking any notice whether it felt right. Someone with whom is part of a spiritual group whom I regard with respect. This day we went out to lunch there were four of us. Chatting as usual about all sorts of things, including going to England this year. Because Mike and I were wondering whether we ought to go over to Britain to see family or take up another pet sitting assignment. It was then one of the ladies said I think you ought to go to Britain to see your brother I feel it's important and what did I do? Instead of sitting with it and meditating, I rushed home to my husband, he was sitting at the computer looking at house sitting assignments and I said straight away I think we should go the Britain! And because at that time he loved it over there he agreed. It was May so I went on line a booked a flight for July 9th over the internet. What followed next was very interesting, but a big lessons also. I went to the doctors for my blood test and there was a queue and I had an appoint elsewhere which was for 9.30 so I was there for 8.30, plenty of time I thought, the nurse certainly was taking her time and about 9.15 I thought how many more people, because it seemed like others were coming in and being seen to after me. Added to the conversation was a young women who came in after me said 'she's a bit slow' I thought I will have a look see how far down the list I was, there were three more before me according to were the paperwork was. So I did something which was out of character and that was put my paper on top. The nurse came in looked at the paper with my name on and said who this is? I said its mine and she look and said Mr so and so weren't you next. GOT CAUGHT OUT in my embarrassment I took the paper off the nurse and couldn't get out quick enough and went to my appointment. Later on that week I thought rather than go back to the nurse at the doctor's surgery I would use the community nurse, so off I went. And guess what she wasn't on that morning and it didn't come as a surprise as that was my gut feeling walking up those stairs. Eventually I had to go back to the nurse at the doctors. And I knew I should have apologised for my manner, but couldn't the words just wouldn't come out my mouth. A month later I was troubled by a sinister looking spot on my right shin, which was painful to touch but couldn't be squeezed, after a month I became worried and went to the doctors. He told me to make an appointment for cut and stitch as it had to be cut out at the doctors and then a few weeks after that which was the Saturday before we were due to leave on the following Wednesday to fly out to Britain on the Friday. I started to get a flashes in the back of my eye and floaty bits in my eye. And my eldest daughter Face-Timed me that night from England so I just mentioned it in passing as I wasn't too concerned she said 'mum get yourself to the hospital straight away'. *(She worked at an opticians)* we send people straight to the hospital when this happens. I put the phone down and my husband drove me to the country hospital. The doctor on duty then sent us to Sydney the next day a seven hour drive, we took some overnight things just in case it got too late to travel back in one day. We arrived about 2.30pm and saw the eye specialist at about 6.30pm. He gave us the OK to fly and to get the eye checked in 6 weeks or so.

We started our journey on the Wednesday, seven hours back up to Sydney, met our daughter Kate for dinner that night because she had work in Sydney that week before flying the next day.

My heart really wasn't in this trip and I didn't know why, (*feel that is why things kept happening to me in a physical way.* As always we enjoyed precious time with family, but the usual places we visited our old haunts just didn't have the same excitement as before and Mike felt the same. It was rainy days and grey skies most of the time we were there. We however decided to catch up with family in France, we planned to stay for a week go back to my eldest daughter for two days before returning to Australia stopping over in Vietnam for a week. Mike had always wanted to visit Vietnam.

We arrived in Bordeaux France and we were picked up by Mike's niece's husband arriving at their home at ten thirty at night. We were busy chatting for an hour and decided to go to bed. Went upstairs, it was then I remembered I needed to go downstairs to put my tablets in the fridge. It was dark and I was looking for the light switch as everyone had gone to bed and Mike was in the bedroom. Feeling around I just couldn't find the switch and didn't realise the landing was only short and as I turned I stepped into what seemed like an abyss. Went to reach a bannister, but there wasn't one so I put my hand in front of me, there were about twelve wooden steps laid on top of concrete as far as I can remember I took three almighty strides, hit a brick wall with my wrist and my head went full force as my wrist gave way *(broken)* banging my head on a shelf as I went down ending up with severely bruised eyes and grazes to my cheek bones. (*When I look back now I realise I was so lucky it could have been so much worse)* Mikes niece tried to keep me awake whilst her husband rang an ambulance (*fortunately they could speak French fluently*. I couldn't get up and was semi-conscious, I was taken to the local hospital where I was x-rayed head to toe and then transferred to a major hospital, to have screws and k-wires put in. I was allowed home the following day were we managed to enjoy the rest of our holidays albeit with my arm in plaster, so I was pleased it didn't spoil things for everyone else.

Of course I had to see my local GP when I arrived home, as we had to cancel the trip in Vietnam and arrived home a week early. My visit to the doctor's surgery was one I will remember for a long while in fact until I have made my peace with the nurse who takes blood because when she saw me sat there with my arm in plaster, she gave me a look of such contempt I could almost read her mind. But thinking about that one I did deserve it. During those six weeks with the k-wires in I focused more on finishing this book and it also gave me time to reflect and ask the Higher Self why. And it wasn't until the wires came out that it came to me. You see I have had to wait a good many hours each time I have visited places as regards my accident, this has been all about PATIENCE learning the lesson (*seems this is the big one hope I have learnt KARMIC lesson this time and able to move on from it*) And then to realise it in all a part of my SACRED CONTRACT as I have written a good part of this book since I have been out of action. You see this booked was started at least ten years ago, and for the last two years it has been coming to mind that I must get this book finished. We are ending this book with one last thought. We are all children of Father/Mother God, and like children, we have to learn patience and understanding, which can take a lifetime in my experience. But once this is mastered we come from a place of non-judgement of all of life, as everything really is in Divine Order. And you might like to know that I have since made my peace with the nurse involved.

# HERE IS A LIST OF SOME OF THE EXPERIENCES I HAVE ENCOUNTERED OVER THE YEARS, I HOPE YOU ENJOY THE READ.

$\mathcal{E}$NGLAND 1996 It was during the time I was pondering about relocating to Australia with Mike as although it was only initially for a few years it was still a big move it was weighing heavily on my mind.

Our kitchen door was made of clear glass and was always open, being in and out all the time it was easier.

Kate was watching television and I went upstairs to make beds etc. When I came back down the door was a bit awkward to open as one of the bar stools was in the way. I pushed it gently as I didn't want to push it over, without giving it much thought I continued what I was doing and headed back upstairs. This time on returning to the kitchen it was almost closed with the stool pressed up against the glass. This made it extra hard to open and made me stop and think about what was going on. I couldn't open it without knocking over the stool and would need to head outside, down the road through the passage and in through the back door. It was then that the penny dropped. My daughter was still watching television, so there was no way she could have done it and it made me consider the symbolism of the situation. Was I being locked out, or told to stay put? Of course when Mike came home I told him what happened he definitely said "locked out!".

## AUSTRALIA

I was in a shopping centre and used the elevator, stood there on my own. A young man about twenty five years old stepped in He looked so sad and tired. I asked him where he worked. He said he was a baker and had just finished work as though it wasn't important. I told him that it was a very important job, and that my younger brother was a baker, but unfortunately he died at the same age that you are. I saw his face change and take on a more positive stance and he perked up as he left elevator.

## MEDITATION

Meditating with our regular group, a sudden flash came to mind of the same group sat outside an Indian tee pee in meditation. I knew that had happened before in one our lifetimes together.

## REIKI PRACTICE

Reiki practise there were about a dozen of us, suddenly the music was playing it was male singers and the sound of sticks being banged together. And instantly I felt that I had been transported back to another life. Where there were monks singing behind us whilst we were giving healing, afterwards we learned most of us experienced the same vision.

## DRIVING BACK TO MELBOURNE

On the drive back to Melbourne from where our future home was to be built, I could tell Mike was tired. It worried me as it was around a 7 hour drive, but Mike being Mike didn't want me to have to drive. Three and a half hours from Melbourne a brilliant beam was shining down on the wind screen, it was very direct and stayed with us for three hours which kept both of us interested, it left us when we only had thirty minutes driving left. My husband said in all these years of driving, (*he was fifty nine*) he had never seen anything like it before. I must add that I closed my eyes during the drive and saw three spheres of emerald green, it was beautiful.

## WASHING MACHINE

One morning the washing machine wouldn't work, they are all computerised these days and it was getting old. So this time I decided to call on the Archangel Michael and use two Reiki symbols over the machine with the palm of my hand still facing the computer part, and asked Michael to fix it. (*Angels know the symbols and the more you use them the better the effect*) *to* my amazement the electronics struck up for a little while, so I did the same again, electronics did it again. This time I calmed myself and took several deep breathes and did it once more and my washing machine started working. I said thank you to the Archangel Michael and his band of Angels, they really like it when you say thank you.

## BUDDHA

During our Friday group meditation, one of the ladies went into some sort of trance, and our teacher took care of things in a loving way but unfortunately it frightened a few of us, as we weren't expecting it.

The next day at home in my meditation room, I opened my Doreen Virtue book titled 'Archangels and Ascended Master' and let it fall open and it was Matrayea (Buddha).

I decided to meditate to connect to him, and asked why I was frightened, he answered me by saying 'Enlightened one the fear you felt was because you did not trust' a healing occurred of a spiritual form. He then said, "So what have you learned?" I replied, "To trust and not to fear". No sooner had I said that that Buddha said to me, "Now go enlightened one, enjoy your humaneness and go and play" waving his hand.

## ABBEY –

Abbey a daughter of a friend of ours who was about 6yrs old at the time seemed very connected to me and loves crystals. We decided to do a little guided meditation together. After I asked her to draw what she saw in her meditation. It was a balloon tied to her wrist, with a rainbow light going through the balloon. Her mother told me she saw Abbey place her hand on her brothers back, when her mother asked her what she was doing. Abbey said, '*Angie does it*' this was a beautiful moment, as the intention was there to heal, and what a beautiful thing for a six year old to do for her younger brother.

## MONTEL SHOW

I was watching the Montel show one afternoon on my own, and he was interviewing Sylvia Browne a renowned clairvoyant, it was then I notice an Angel doing somersaults inside a white Orb around her, the orb was about eight inches. It was really very beautiful, just a pity I had no one to share it with.

## REIKI

Whilst giving my daughter Kate a Reiki, our little dog Jack followed us into the room and attempted to lay down under the table and it was then he was lifted up by his back legs we couldn't see by whom and was led out the room on his two front legs and he didn't object. This time Kate saw it for herself.

## RING ROAD

The ring road as we now call it. My husband and I were travelling towards Melbourne and doing something I don't normally do and that is take my rings off and placing them on my lap to rub hand cream onto my hands. At that moment steam was oozing out of the bonnet of the car so we pulled into a layby which was laid with gravel. We both jumped out not realising my rings were on my knee we called for the break-down truck who towed us to his garage some 15 kilometers away. We then had to wait 3hrs for a good friend to pick us up this is when I realised my rings were missing. The next day we continued our journey Melbourne albeit in the ute and stopped at the place I lost the rings knowing that there was slim chance of ever finding them as trucks and cars had pulled in after we left. We got out the ute at the same spot my husband went looking further up and it was then as I stood I called upon Angels help I had no sooner said 'thank you' when for some unknow reason I looked down at my feet and I saw something catch my eye only a small glitter at the tip of my toes gently moving some gravel to one side there they were both rings truly amazing everytime we pass that area we call it the ring road.

If I were to offer you all words of wisdom I would like to say;
Honour and Validate Your Own Feelings
Speak Your Truth from your Heart
Live Your Truth from your Heart
And most importantly be True to Yourself

JUST NOW THAT AS YOU WALK FORWARD IN LIFE THE ANGELS KNOW EXACTLY WHERE YOU ARE GOING TO PUT YOUR FOOT DOWN BEFORE YOU DO. TALK TO THEM REGULAR ASK THEM TO HELP YOU AS THEY WILL NOT IMPOSE ON YOUR FREE WILL.

LOVE LIGHT AND MANY BLESSINGS

*Angie Gabriel*

Printed in the United States
By Bookmasters